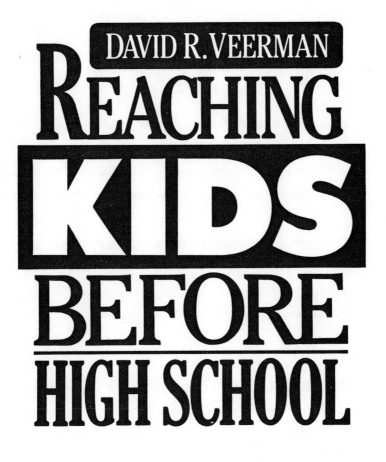

DAVID R. VEERMAN

REACHING KIDS BEFORE HIGH SCHOOL

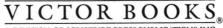

VICTOR BOOKS®

A DIVISION OF SCRIPTURE PRESS PUBLICATIONS INC.
USA CANADA ENGLAND

Library of Congress Cataloging-In-Publication Data

Veerman, David.
    Reaching kids before high school / by David Veerman.
        p.   c.m.
    Includes bibliographical references.
    ISBN 0-89693-519-1
    1. Church work with teenagers.   2. Junior high school students — United States — Religious life.   I. Title.
  BV4447.V39   1990
  259'.23 — dc20   90-33532
                                                          CIP

CONTENTS

85417

DEDICATION

*To the "Veerman women" — Gail, Kara, and Dana,
who give me much more love, understanding, support,
and encouragement than I deserve.*

ACKNOWLEDGMENTS

Special thanks to the following youth ministry experts who took time to read the manuscript and offer invaluable guidance and suggestions.

Dr. Bruce B. Barton, President of The Livingstone Corporation

Richard Dunn, Chairman of the Department of Youth Ministry, Trinity College (Deerfield, Illinois)

Dr. James Galvin, Vice President of The Livingstone Corporation

Greg Johnson, Editor of Breakaway *Magazine (Focus on the Family)*

The Rev. Tim Kirk, Associate Pastor of Naperville Presbyterian Church (Naperville, Illinois)

Laura Laffoon, National Campus Life/JV Coordinator for Youth for Christ/USA

Greg Lafferty, Junior High Minister of Wheaton Bible Church (Wheaton, Illinois)

Scott Pederson, Director of Sonlight Express of Willow Creek Community Church (South Barrington, Illinois)

Len Woods, Editor of Youthwalk *(Walk Thru the Bible Ministries)*

CHAPTER 1

"JUNIOR HIGHERS?
YOU'VE GOT TO BE KIDDING!"

"You've got to be kidding!" she almost shouted back to me in the church foyer. You would have thought that I had pressured her for a large donation to the building fund, urged her to preach, or inquired about a personal matter. But I had only asked if she would consider helping teach the junior high Sunday School class.

I shouldn't have been surprised. Even professional youth workers cringe when they hear the words "junior highers." The mental image is the "Tasmanian Devil" of Bugs Bunny cartoons—a whirling tornado of unlimited energy, boundless curiosity, and ravenous appetite, devastating everything and everybody in its path. This caricature arises from our memories of junior high; it is further reinforced by our observations of kids at church or in the neighborhood; and it is finally confirmed by our own children as they enter adolescence.

Ask a group of adults what they remember about junior high (sixth, seventh, and eighth grades), and you'll get an earful. Painful memories flood many—struggles with peers, popularity, pimples, and puberty. Others remember physical frustrations as they coped with growth or lack of it—cherubic boys yearning to be bigger and taller, and gangly girls wishing they could shrink.

OUR RECOLLECTIONS

"Quiet!" With his face contorted in anger, Mr. Jackson whirled from the blackboard and slammed his fist on the desk. A momentary hush fell over the classroom, but the whispers, notes, and flying objects resumed as soon as he turned back to the board.

We tormented that poor algebra teacher all year. He could not control us, and we knew it. In fact, during one class period, he said "quiet" 63 times. I know; we counted—out loud.

That's one of my vivid junior high memories.

Jean, 45, recalled the day she lowered a friend out of the school window so she could run to the store for candy.

Frank, 36, remembered fighting constantly to prove how tough he was.

Betsy, 40, recalled "getting her period" and the embarrassment of pimples.

"All of nostalgia isn't pleasant, however. For many junior high was a tough time, and digging up those memories can be painful. Let's face it—many of us would just as soon forget that we ever experienced junior high. Which may be one reason why many adults steer away from working with junior high kids, the supposed armpit of youth ministry. For this very reason, though, it's probably helpful to deal with our junior high experiences. Understanding our own wounds may be the very thing that enriches our ministry to the new generation of junior highers."

From "Focus on Junior High" by Steve Dickie, *Youthworker Journal,* Winter 1989.

I also remember going from 140 to 170 pounds in one year, throwing an egg at a car to be accepted by the popular kids in my new neighborhood, and trying desperately to impress certain girls.

The stories could go on and on. No wonder adults are wary of getting involved with this age-group.

OUR RESPONSES

Remembering vividly the painful moments of the junior high years, adults respond in various ways to the real, live junior highers in their world.

1. *Harangue*

Some adults react to junior highers with judgment and criticism. Seeing the eighth-grade girls write and pass notes during the worship service or seeing the sixth-grade boys run through the sanctuary afterward, they shake their heads and criticize.

"I can see from their faces that Beth and Kara really want to be here," commented a young father sarcastically to my wife one Sunday.

Your day is coming, she answered silently as she thought of his seven-year-old son.

Others complain to parents and principals and write vitriolic letters about neighborhood mischief. They also point judgmental fingers and comment about "kids today" to anyone who'll listen.

It's easy to criticize and complain, because early adolescents always seem to be getting into trouble, acting silly, or displaying bad attitudes. They are visible targets.

2. *Hide (and don't seek)*

Some adults respond to junior highers by ignoring them, acting as though they don't exist. Babies are "darling," and are smothered with "cootchy-coos" and kisses. Toddlers and preschoolers look and sound so cute, and are complimented on their physical progress. Even grade school children receive loads of attention from doting grandparents, church members, neighbors, and family friends. But around sixth grade, children become "invisible." Adults often avoid them, acting as though they aren't there.

"Most people feel totally unequipped to work with kids in the age group where the maturity levels span the spectrum between Transformers and Trojans. All it really takes, however, is someone who will *love them* in the midst of all their diversity, and someone who will look at the big picture and wait for God to bear fruit in His time, not theirs."

Greg Johnson, Editor of *Breakaway* (Focus on the Family's junior high magazine).

Mark Twain is reported to have recommended humorously to put children in barrels and feed them through the knotholes; then, when they reach adolescence, to close up the holes!

Many people respond that way—avoiding, ignoring, sealing off junior highers—virtually "hiding" and pretending that they don't exist. That's why the junior high age-group is one of the most neglected in the church. There are programs for almost everyone else, from babies to senior citizens. Singles, young couples, parents, and older adults have a smorgasbord of activities from which to choose. And when a youth director arrives, his or her commission is usually to work with the high schoolers (and perhaps advise the junior high sponsors).

Those who "hide" leapfrog over the junior high years. (And, by the way, when these kids are ignored, they tend to act up even more, doing almost anything to be noticed.)

3. *Hope*

This reaction is similar to "hiding," but relates more to parents. Nothing strikes fear into a parent's heart more than having his or her oldest child about to enter junior high school. (I'll discuss this more in chapter 4.) These parents have read about teenagers; they've heard stories; and they're scared to death.

Often they talk as though early adolescence is just another stage through which their children must pass, like thumb sucking or the "terrible twos," and they hope their kids will survive.

These parents tend to withdraw, treating older children with benign neglect while hoping for the best.

Unfortunately, this reaction can blind parents to their young teens' problems and related symptoms. Junior highers who experiment with drugs or alcohol or sex are not experts at camouflaging their actions. Mom and Dad are often shocked when the habits come to light because they haven't seen the obvious signs.

● Ken brags about how he can sneak off to do whatever he wants.

● Celeste laughs about how her mom believes anything Celeste tells her.

● Keri is a model child at home and at church, but she is a terror at school.

Simply hoping for the best is foolish and irresponsible.

4. Hire

Another response to the presence of junior highers at church or in our families is to employ a professional youth worker to deal with them. (Few churches do this.) Aware of the problems and pressures of early adolescence, concerned adults believe that the only answer is to hire someone who has been specially trained in working with this difficult age. The profile for the youth worker usually includes the following: young, good-looking, athletic, musical, funny, creative, spiritual, intelligent, firm, married, and willing to work for peanuts—a combination of Michael Jordan, Mother Teresa, Steven Spielberg, Amy Grant, and Bill Cosby. This per-

---

"Never mind the youth director's philosophy of ministry, stated objectives, creative programming, or well-intentioned efforts. *When evaluating their church's youth group, the bottom line for most parents is, 'Does my child enjoy it?'* "

Clayton Baumann, Executive Director, North Area Youth for Christ (Chicago suburbs).

son is expected to attract, entertain, teach, discipline, and lead young people to Christ and spiritual maturity—a most unrealistic task.

On the positive side, adults who respond this way are aware of and very sensitive to the needs of this age-group. They will form a powerful lobbying influence within the church, forcing church leaders to remember junior highers when setting the budget or adding staff.

The problem with this response, however, is that it assumes a person can be found who meets the ideal profile and that one person will be able to minister to all the kids in the group. In reality, every child is different and represents a unique set of challenges and opportunities. Unrealistic expectations for those we hire usually result in discouragement, disappointment, or disillusionment.

Another problem with this response is that it pushes the responsibility onto other people, assuming that "they" are more qualified and will be more effective than we could be. Actually, this is a common North American reaction, thinking that we can hire a specialist to cover any situation or throw money at a problem to solve it, while we sit and watch. Professionals can offer great expertise, and money certainly helps, but human beings and their problems are more complex than any simple solution.

"It is clear that youth ministry is vital to a church's overall growth. Church staff and families in growing churches know that a strong youth ministry attracts young people, parents and families with young children.

"Growing churches pay a lot of attention to youth ministry. Because of that, they're the ones confronting the challenges of growth instead of decline."

From "Youth Ministry: Its Impact on Church Growth" by Jolene L. Roehlepartain, *Group Magazine*, September 1989.

5. *Help*

The final response simply says, "What can I do to help?" Obviously this is my punch line—the response I was getting to and the one I endorse.

Adults who care about the junior high or middle school children in their churches, families, or neighborhoods can have a significant ministry with these young people in a variety of ways. Instead of criticizing or avoiding them or expecting someone else to do everything, they can . . .

- Pray—for the early adolescents they know, for their parents, and for those who are ministering to them.
- Affirm—the junior highers they know, greeting them by name and offering compliments whenever possible.
- Assist—those who carry the main ministry load, by driving, phoning, collecting props for meetings, and doing other necessary tasks.
- Reach out—directly to young people by teaching a Sunday School class, counseling at a camp or retreat, sponsoring a youth group, leading a small group, or spending time with certain junior highers.
- Lead—by organizing a junior high ministry team at church, a parents' council, a neighborhood youth group, and so forth, and by being an advocate for junior high ministry.

> "Junior high ministry is important. It is also demanding. If you do it, you will be stretched like never before. You will also lose your mind. (How do you think I lost mine?)"
>
> Len Woods, Editor of *Youthwalk* (a teenage devotional guide published by Walk Thru the Bible Ministries).

Think again about your junior high years. What adults played a significant, positive role in your life? And what did they *do* that you still remember today? You can be that kind of person for the early adolescents around you.

THINK IT THROUGH

1. What kind of person were you in junior high or middle school (sixth, seventh, and eighth grades)?

2. Describe a negative experience from those years.

3. Describe a positive experience from those years.

4. List the names of the early adolescents you know.

5. Which word best describes your response to this age-group (circle one): harangue, hide, hope, hire, help.

   Explain.

6. In what ways would you like to help minister to the junior highers in your world?

CHAPTER 2

AT THE CROSSROADS

- With bright eyes shining, Traci could hardly wait for third grade to begin. Miss Kramer made learning an exciting adventure (she was "the best teacher in the world!"), textbooks opened a new world, and all of Traci's friends were with her in school. As the elementary years passed, Traci didn't even mind doing homework, although she needed occasional proddings from Mom and Dad. She was a model daughter and student. That was four years ago. Today, Traci is into hard rock, she has painted her room black and her hair blue, and she hangs out with troubled kids at school. Arguing constantly with her parents, Traci has thought and talked about running away.
- He seemed shy, but when you got to know Jeff, you discovered a pleasant personality and a great sense of humor. Jeff was a good student, especially in fourth grade when he won awards in science and English. He's in eighth grade now—just barely, after taking math again in summer school.

17

• "King of the Playground" was Michael's nickname. He could run faster, jump higher, and throw a ball farther than anyone else in school, even the boys in the next grade. Michael looked older, and he walked the halls with a self-assured confidence. Everyone knew he was destined for stardom. But today, Michael just hangs around the playgrounds. He should be a junior in high school, but he dropped out—after being suspended several times for fighting during the last few years.

What made the difference in each of these young lives? What did they have in common? What changed Traci, Jeff, and Michael from optimistic, happy, and fun-loving children into sullen and rebellious teenagers? The answer—their junior high experience.

These are the crossroads years where young people choose paths that can change their lives. These years are crucial for physical, emotional, moral, mental, social, and spiritual development. According to an article by Susan Tifft in *Time* magazine (June 26, 1989, p. 51), "Television calls them the wonder years, but for millions of youths between the ages of 10 and 15, the years of early adolescence are anything but wonderful. No longer children, not quite adults, they are bombarded by dizzying physical

---

"You can see the lights going out. It seems to happen somewhere in junior high. A child goes in soft and comes out hard. He enters laughing and innocent . . . he leaves unsmiling and jaded. The eclipse shouldn't come so fast, so soon. But it does.

"The moral crossroads that used to come in college or high school have moved to junior high, to middle school. By eighth grade, a young person will probably have to decide about his first drink, his first drugs, his first sexual experience. One out of five will have sex *before* they enter high school."

Ron Hutchcraft, New York Area Director of Youth for Christ.

changes, reeling emotions, and raging hormones. Today's youngsters, however, face problems far more formidable than acne or gangly limbs. Drinking, drug abuse, sexually transmitted diseases, and teenage pregnancy, once the province of high schools, have drifted into the lower grades."

The pressures and problems that we faced in college or high school are now the struggles of much younger kids. It is a generation at risk. Let's take a closer look at what junior highers are facing.

THEY ARE "RUSHED"

As we ate dinner one October afternoon, my second-grader laughed and said, "She was probably on drugs." It was just a passing comment—she didn't mean anything by it, but I almost fell out of my chair. During my *high school* years, we hardly ever heard of drugs. They may have been used by people in crime areas of big cities far away, but not in our town, or by anyone we knew. But my grade school daughter had just made a casual reference to drugs, as a natural part of conversation.

Today, grade schoolers know all about drugs and why they shouldn't take them—and who does. They know about child abuse, AIDS, and dangerous strangers. They see warnings on TV, hear them on the radio, read them in magazines, and hear them in the classroom. In this age of information, they are barraged with news reports, warnings, educational programs, and special bulletins.

Don't get me wrong. I think we should put pictures of missing kids on milk cartons and trucks, educate children about the "bad guys" out there, and participate in "Neighborhood Watch." These are the helpful, positive benefits of high tech communication. But a negative result is the loss of innocence for children. Even before they can talk, they learn that the world is a frightening and dangerous place in which to live. The "boogeyman" is real.

Add to the helpful communiques the usual television fare of sex and violence, the lurid lyrics of popular music, and the twisted values of many videos and movies, and you see the massive assault on young hearts and minds.

"Adolescence is not a mistake—it is a perfection! It is an exact and perfect stage of growth and development that is the period of changing from child to adult. The very features of adolescence that are so frustrating to parents and adolescents themselves—adolescent illusions of greatness, the adolescent preoccupation with freedom and independence—these features are the way they are because the Great Creator, in His infinite wisdom and unlimited power, has designed adolescence as an ideal, final preparation for adulthood."

From *You Can Enjoy Your Teen* by Dr. Jim Geddes (Old Tappan, N.J.: Fleming H. Revell, 1989).

Kids are also rushed by parents and the educational system. There are music lessons, classes for gifted students, sports teams, and camps for every age. For many families, school and play have become serious business.

Dealing with adult problems at their tender age and being pushed to accelerate their pace of learning, our children are forced to grow up too fast.

THEY ARE PRESSURED AND TEMPTED

Children today also face pressures unheard of in previous generations. North America is in the throes of a drug and alcohol epidemic, and substance abusers are younger and younger. A 1983 study by the Search Institute of Minneapolis reported that 26 percent of high school seniors had their first experience with alcohol in the seventh grade or earlier. In sharp contrast, 56 percent of eighth-graders reported having their first drink of alcohol in the seventh grade or earlier. This is a major difference, with a rate of seventh grade or earlier use by eighth-graders double that of high school seniors.

In a study of students from Minnesota and Colorado, Search Institute also found that:

- nearly all eighth-graders had some experience with alcohol.
- 1 out of 3 had used an illicit drug.
- 1 out of 4 had used alcohol 20 or more times.
- 1 out of 6 had had more than five drinks in the two weeks preceding the survey.

Furthermore, after surveying 8,000 fifth- through ninth-grade American students who indicated that they were active in a church, parish, or synagogue, Search Institute reported that:

- 1 out of 4 fifth- and sixth-graders had used alcohol in the last 12 months.
- 1 out of 10 sixth-graders had gotten drunk at least once in the last year.

Young people also feel pressure to be sexually active. Consider the typical plots for many television shows; broken marriages, adultery, and assorted affairs are assumed to be a natural part of life. Movies and videos are even worse, displaying as PG or PG-13 what just a few years ago was considered pornographic.

MTV and other music video outlets also play a major role in influencing our children. Since the '50s, rock 'n roll has been a dominant force in youth culture. Before MTV, only a handful of young people on any high school or junior high campus became devoted followers of rock stars. They could buy records, hear songs on the radio, watch an occasional appearance on television, and perhaps attend a concert of their favorite artist. Today, however, musicians will perform in our homes at the push of a button, allowing us to see their antics and hear their messages over and over. And rock stars seem to try to outdo each other in sexual explicitness, obscenities, and outrageousness.

In addition, many of the rock radio stations feature disc jockeys who major in dirty talk and double meanings. It's called "trash radio," and it's on the rise. Young people love music and are attracted by this kind of shock humor—and they are influenced by what they hear.

This tremendous emphasis on sex is having an effect. According to a study by the Allan Guttmacher Institute, 7 million boys and 5 million girls between the ages of 13 and 19 are sexually active. Each year, 1.1 million teenage girls become pregnant; 30,000 of these girls are under the age of 15. And studies by the Search Institute indicate that 15 percent of seventh-graders and 18 percent of eighth-graders will have sexual intercourse one or more times this year.

Because young people see and hear so much about drinking, drugs, and sex, they tend to see those activities as "normal," and are more apt to give in. But the greatest pressure comes from peers. Wanting to be accepted and to be more adultlike, early adolescents are quite vulnerable to the well worn line, "Everybody's doing it." No one wants to be outside of the crowd.

THEY ARE GROWING

Early adolescence marks a time of tremendous growth for our children, in just about every area of life.

Physical Growth
The junior high years bring on rapid physical development, the most obvious area of growth. This development happens earlier for girls than for boys. And there is usually a "growth spurt." (Earlier I mentioned that I gained 30 pounds in one year.) This growth

---

"Girls go through puberty like Grant took Richmond, alternating screaming laughter with screaming hysteria, interspersed with sullen silences when 'she' (meaning me, her mother) comes into the room. Girls of 13 are already conscious of the fact that they have a figure and that it, like a really good lawn, will need life-long maintenance. They 'diet' by skipping dinner and munch a lettuce leaf while the family gorges. They balance this with telling sympathetic friends over after-school pizza or french fries that 'she' never serves anything but starches."

From "Nearing Adulthood, or: Why You'd Hate to Be 13 Again" by Janet Cool, *Chicago Tribune*, Tuesday, January 24, 1989.

produces enormous appetites, a lack of coordination, awkward-ness, self-consciousness, and alternating periods of energy and fatigue. And these physical changes can wreak havoc with a young person's self-concept.

The junior high years also mark a growth in sexual awareness. Puberty begins at 10+ for girls and 11+ for boys. Sex organs develop, voices change, pubic hair appears, pimples pop out, and hormones rampage. Usually this is when boys begin to masturbate, leading to feelings of confusion and guilt. A new awareness of the opposite sex and an obsession with one's own body develops. Boys begin to wonder if they'll ever get taller, girls wonder if they'll ever stop growing, and both spend hours in front of the mirror.

Intellectual Growth

Jean Piaget (1896–1980), an eminent Swiss psychologist famous for his studies of the thought processes of children, identified four stages of a child's cognitive development. Children (ages 7–11) in stage 3, the "concrete operations stage," don't think abstractly or conceptually. Instead, they think more in terms of the concrete and cause and effect. Children (11 and up) in stage 4, the "formal operations" stage, begin to use logic and to think in terms of concepts and abstract ideas. Junior highers are in transition mentally, learning to learn and learning to think abstractly.

School can be an exhilarating or discouraging experience as students are presented with an array of facts and concepts. Dur-

---

"The nation's middle and junior high schools—encompassing grades 6 through 9—play a potentially crucial role in shaping the future of young adolescents. Yet these institutions have largely been left out of a flurry of educational reforms that have focused on U.S. elementary and secondary schools over the past several years."

Susan Tifft, *Time* magazine, June 26, 1989.

ing these years, certain students may jump ahead, discovering the world of ideas, opening their imaginations, and understanding the potential results of their choices and actions. But others may be left behind, ignored by teachers who gravitate toward the "brighter" students.

The educational process for many young people is like explaining how to operate a computer to a jungle tribesman. He may hear what you are saying, memorize the parts, and even understand how the machine works, but he still will be confused because the whole discussion is out of his context. In the same way, early adolescents don't have the context of life experience and perspective to be able to understand fully all that they are being taught.

As an assignment for a class I was teaching at Wheaton College, two female students (from Indiana and Wisconsin) interviewed two twelve-year-old girls at a mall. These junior high girls shared freely about their boyfriends, sex, and their thoughts of marriage. Suddenly one of the girls turned to my student and said, "Do they have television in Wisconsin?" This girl knew all about sex and was even talking about marriage, but she knew very little about life.

In my junior high Sunday School class we were discussing Jesus' confrontation with the Gadarene demoniac—the Bible describes him as being a wild man, with broken chains hanging off his arms because "no man could hold him." As I described what must have been a frightening scene to the disciples, one of the boys exclaimed, "Why didn't they shoot him?" This young man had not been able to put the story into its historical context. Early adolescence is a time of intellectual transition and growth.

Social Growth

Junior highers are also growing and changing socially. In elementary school, my best friend lived next door, and we did everything together. But when I went to junior high school, we drifted apart, mainly because he was held back to repeat sixth grade.

My experience is typical for that age. During grade school, a child's friends can be found in the neighborhood, because his or her mobility is limited and the school is probably nearby. In junior high, however, those friendships begin to change, centering more on common interests and activities.

Early adolescents can seem obsessed with their friends, forming tight cliques, writing copious notes, and talking incessantly on the phone. Friends are important because fragile egos need acceptance, affirmation, and a place to belong. And while young people feel almost desperate to be part of a group, they can be very cruel to those who are different or outside their circle of friends. I've heard kids gang up on an individual and mock him unmercifully. It's as though they have to protect themselves by lashing out at others. Some people never quite recover from those verbal beatings, carrying scars in their psyche for life.

Another changing social area for young people is their relationships with adults. Junior highers want to be treated as "older," to have more freedom, and to make their own decisions. This push for independence may lead to heated arguments with Mom and Dad. At the same time, however, most still tend to be very family oriented. In their major study, Merton and Irene Strommen found that early adolescents had a strong desire for a close family. (See *Five Cries of Parents:* Harper and Row, 1985.) And junior highers will listen to adults and even obey teachers, coaches, youth leaders, and other authorities if spoken to firmly and not in anger.

Early adolescents are very vulnerable socially. All their feelings and frustrations from the changes in their lives seem to be focused in this area.

Psychological Growth
According to Erik Erikson's classic stages of psychological development, the focus of the "school age" (approximately ages 6–12) is "industry versus inferiority." "Industry" means a sense of competence. In other words, the child needs to feel that he or she is good at something.

In the next stage, "adolescence" (approximately ages 13–18), the focus is "identity versus confusion." Here the young person is working on self-concept and answering the questions, "Who am I? And where do I fit in?"

Top Twenty Worries of American Young Adolescents

1. School performance	57%
2. About my looks	53%
3. How well other kids like me	48%
4. Parent might die	47%
5. How my friends treat me	45%
6. Hunger and poverty in U.S.	38%
7. Violence in U.S.	36%
8. Might lose best friend	36%
9. Drugs and drinking	35%
10. Might not get good job	30%
11. Physical development	26%
12. Nuclear destruction of U.S.	25%
13. Parents might divorce	22%
14. That I may die soon	21%
15. Sexual abuse	19%
16. Friends will get me in trouble	18%
17. Drinking by a parent	15%
18. Getting beat up at school	12%
19. Physical abuse by parent	12%
20. That I might kill myself	12%

From *Five Cries of Parents* by Merton P. and A. Irene Strommen (San Francisco: Harper and Row, 1985).

Although the timing of these two stages varies widely, it is clear that *early* adolescence falls right in the middle of them. Thus, most junior highers, especially the younger ones, will be experimenting, trying athletics, music, art, and other school activities, and working on their life skills. They want a sense of accomplishment. And some of the older ones will be trying on different identities, attempting to discover and understand who they are. "Am I an athlete?" "Am I a leader?" "Am I good-looking?" "Am I smart?" "Am I shy?" These struggles consume much of a young person's emotional energy.

Incidentally, because young adolescents haven't fully developed their identities, most programs designed for high school students will not be effective with them. Instead, junior highers need activities and classes that will help them accomplish and achieve, to feel competent. Using high school programs with junior highers (or combining both groups) is a mistake.

The avalanche of changes also affects their emotions, and the ups and downs can be extreme. One of the causes for the emotional roller coaster is physical, as hormones flow through the system. In addition, there are mental, psychological, social, and physical factors. Kids fear rejection, and often feel misunderstood, left out, ugly, and stupid. How would you feel if the girl you liked was a foot taller than you, your friends called you "runt," and the teacher laughed when he asked you to stand up? Or consider your elation when you discover through your best friend Jolene that Brett (the totally good-looking new guy) likes you.

Early adolescents, especially girls, let you know how they feel. And their emotions indicate what is going on inside.

Spiritual Growth

Let's face it. It's just not "cool" to talk about God in junior high. For kids trying to grow up, religion is often seen as something for little children or religious types. Many churches have confirmation or catechism classes for children. The purpose of these classes is to teach church doctrine and to "confirm" them in the faith. Ironically, however, confirmation often leads to a quick exit from church. It's as though the parental pressure comes off and the young person says: "All right. I went to the classes for you. Now that it's over, I'll do what *I* want to do."

One of the problems is that these classes tend to be very conceptual and irrelevant, and thus, extremely boring. Students may memorize Bible verses and creeds, but often they don't understand what the verses and creeds mean or how they fit into their lives. Junior highers need to see how faith makes a difference in the real world. They need to see models of faith, and they need a place where they can voice their doubts and disbelief.

For those outside the influence of any local church (which

includes the vast majority of early adolescents), the spiritual realm can seem quite fuzzy. They may wonder about God or become curious about the occult. But whatever their background or interest, they are biblically illiterate. (This is true for many church kids too.)

There is a growing gap between the evangelical world and the

Biggest Problem Facing Teenagers

	1987	1985	1983	1977
Drug abuse	54%	40%	35%	27%
Alcohol abuse	12	14	10	7
Teenage pregnancy	11	3	—	—
Peer pressure	10	8	8	5
AIDS	5	—	—	—
Getting along with parents	2	2	5	20
Problems in growing up	2	5	1	6
Unemployment	2	8	16	6
Teenage suicide	2	3	—	—
School problems	1	4	5	3
Financing college	1	3	1	—
Fear of war	1	2	4	—
Economic problems	1	3	2	3
Career uncertainties	—	—	3	3
Miscellaneous	5	7	5	12
Don't know	8	13	18	14
	117*	115*	113*	106*

* Columns add up to more than 100% because some teens named more than one problem.

Young people were asked to name their biggest problem.

From the Gallup Study, *America's Youth, 1977–1988* (Princeton, N.J.: The Gallup Organization, 1988).

rest of society, which is becoming increasingly secular. This secularization is obvious in the younger generation. In sixth grade, my daughter invited one of her friends to attend church with us. Amy came from a nice suburban family. I had spoken with her father and knew that his background was Lutheran. But after the service, Amy said that it was the first time she had ever gone to church. And this happened in one of the most "churched" communities in America.

Most early adolescents live in a spiritual vacuum. They are hungry for something, but don't know why or what to do about their hunger.

THE CHALLENGE

Why should we minister to junior highers? Because . . .

- they are thinking through "adult" issues although they are still children; they need adults who will accept them, affirm them, and let them enjoy life.
- they are experiencing tremendous physical changes which can be very confusing; they need support and encouragement.
- they are at an age of personality and character formation; what better time to reach young people for Christ?
- they are under increasing academic and moral pressure; they are vulnerable and need support.
- they are forming values and asking questions about life; they need answers from God's Word.
- they are very impressionable and still accept adults as models for lifestyle and values; they need us to offer friendship, love, and positive role models.
- they are going to the same heaven or hell as adults; they need Christ.

Junior highers desperately need help navigating through these difficult years. They need concerned and caring adults who will spend time listening, loving, watching, and teaching them—and lead them to Christ.

Are you that kind of person? Will you take the challenge?

THINK IT THROUGH

1. What evidence have you seen recently to support the statement that children are "hurried"?

2. What are the most popular teenage radio stations in your area? List three of the top ten songs on the pop charts right now.

3. Which junior highs and middle schools do the early adolescents in your church attend?

4. What temptations might a junior higher face in a typical school day?

5. Imagine that a young person shares a problem with you that he or she is facing. Describe what that problem might be.

6. What might you say to help or encourage him or her?

7. What young people might possibly come to you for help? Why?

C H A P T E R 3

"NOW WHAT DO WE DO?"

PARABLE

Since as far back as he could remember, John wanted to
be a builder. During childhood, his daydreamed
occupations included carpenter, architect, general
contractor, civil engineer, bricklayer — his imagination
catapulting him into each newly discovered construction
opportunity. And although John's adult career track had
taken a different direction, still he harbored
that secret ambition.

Then one day he saw that he had the chance to realize
those childhood dreams. There was time (two weeks of
vacation); there was space (his backyard); and there was
money (his special projects funds were ample). So, after a
trip to the lumberyard, selecting only the finest wood,
nails, and other supplies, John gathered his
tools and began to build.

Measuring, sawing, and nailing, John worked as one
obsessed, stopping only for food and sleep. Slowly his
dream rose and spread across the yard. *I'm a builder!*

he thought as he fell into bed each night, exhausted but exhilarated by the idea.

Of course John's project was the talk of the neighborhood. The sights, sounds, and obvious expense were impressive. Then, after two weeks, the hammering subsided, and John's neighbors gathered at his fence to look and comment on his project.

"He sure worked hard," said one.

"What dedication!" said another.

"And I don't think I've ever seen such wonderful workmanship," added a third.

"Just look at those beautiful boards!" said someone else.

"BUT WHAT IS IT?" they thought. And no one knew—not even John.

The moral of this story: Before you begin, be sure you know what you're building.

PREAMBLE

Assuming that you are convinced of the need for ministering to early adolescents and of your ability to play a significant role in that ministry, the next step is to think through what you hope to accomplish. It may seem obvious, but too many youth workers, following their dreams, rush off to buy shiny new supplies and tools and begin working without knowing what they want to build. Their motives are pure, their commitment and dedication are commendable, and their materials are of the highest quality. But the results are amorphous structures, lacking definition and direction.

That's what this chapter is about—helping you develop a purpose and philosophy for your ministry.

PROCESS

Whatever the project or program, it is important that you follow this three-step process: purpose, philosophy, and plan.

Purpose

Simply stated, the purpose is the ultimate goal of your work, what the final product will look like. John wanted to build something, but he wasn't sure *what* he wanted to build. A house, a skyscraper, and a bridge differ greatly in their construction. The kind of structure chosen determines the expense, materials, tools, time, and methods.

> "In a rapidly changing society, when adults are struggling to adapt to a new social order, few adults are genuinely committed to helping teenagers attain a healthy adulthood. Young people are thus denied the special recognition and protection that society previously accorded their age group."
>
> From *All Grown Up and No Place to Go* by Dr. David Elkind (Addison-Wesley Publishing Co., 1984).

The same could be said about youth work. Although it is possible to have more than one goal (or "structure") for a group or specific young person, it is important to spell out each goal individually. Be sure to discuss your goals with church leaders and parents to make sure that you're all heading in the same direction. Possible goals could include: to lead young people to Christ; to help young people grow in their faith; to help early adolescents resist the pressures and temptations of the junior high years; to build within junior highers feelings of competence and self-esteem; to teach young people basic life skills; and so forth.

After choosing a goal (or goals), write a simple purpose statement. If, for example, your goal is evangelism, you could state: "The purpose of this ministry is to help junior high age young people trust Jesus Christ as Saviour."

Of course, in order to decide your goals, you should have a good understanding of the young people with whom you will be working. I work with early adolescents in two very different arenas. At church, I head the junior high ministry team. Because of the setting, the fact that all of the kids profess to be Christians, and the need they have for knowing how their faith applies during this difficult time in their lives, our purpose statement reads: "To help students understand how faith in Jesus Christ should change their lives." Sunday School is the main program already in place to help reach that goal.

We also realize that outreach is important, giving these kids the opportunity to bring their friends to a place where they can hear the Gospel. So another goal of the ministry is: "To motivate and provide opportunities for Christian students to reach their friends for Christ." To help reach this goal, we have a youth group that meets every other week in members' homes, mystery meetings (trips to unannounced locations such as bowling alleys, miniature golf courses, etc.), and special events.

Another purpose statement for our group is: "To teach and encourage young people to serve others." To help meet this goal, we sponsor an annual service project.

But I also work with junior highers in the neighborhood through Campus Life/JV (Youth for Christ's ministry for junior highers). Because this ministry is a direct response to the vast world of non-Christian young people, it's purpose is pre-evangelism and evangelism. The program, then, is designed to address that purpose.

Philosophy
In this step you "identify your ministry nonnegotiables." This means determining what you believe about ministry, young people, and how they should be treated. Your philosophy should be consistent with your purpose. The philosophy of your ministry affects the way you perform your ministry. Your program design should reflect this philosophy, and the curriculum and other materials you use should be consistent with it.

My philosophy of ministry includes the concept that youth ministry must be relational. In other words, leaders should build relationships with young people, spending time in their world, getting to know them, becoming their friend. I also believe that any classes or studies should be practical, showing young people how to apply the Bible to their lives. You can see how these two tenets of my philosophy of ministry would affect my ministry plan.

Plan
The plan is the actual design of the program—what you will do, consistent with your philosophy, that helps you achieve your purposes or goals. Your plan should include how staff members (volunteer and salaried) spend their time; what activities, events, meetings, groups, etc. you will sponsor; and what facilities and materials you will use.

First think through your overall strategy; then plan specific events. Every activity should have an objective. For each event you plan, create a purpose statement explaining how that event ties into your overall ministry goals. Ongoing programs, as well as individual events, should each have an objective.

As I mentioned earlier, the Sunday School program in our church is designed to help us reach our goal of helping young people understand how faith in Christ can change their lives. This purpose is stated in our objective for junior high Sunday School. The objective for each individual class, then, should tie into the overall objective of the Sunday School program. Objectives should be concise, specific, and measurable.

Let's say that I am teaching a Sunday School class, and we are studying the Gospel of Luke. This Sunday we will discuss the story in chapter 17 where Jesus heals the ten lepers, but only one returns to thank Him. My objective could be: "As a result of this lesson, my students will write a 'thank-you list' to use in their prayer time." That objective is specific, action-oriented, and consistent with our purpose for Sunday School.

One of the program objectives of Campus Life/JV is to teach young people life skills, and one of these skills is "How to Make Friends." The topic for the first meeting in this series is "How to Meet Friends." The objective reads: "As a result of this meeting, young people will list 3–5 places to find potential friends." Again, this objective is specific and involves action.

Objectives do not have to be action-oriented. "Knowledge" objectives, in which the focus is on teaching content, can also be effective. One such knowledge objective might be: "As a result of this meeting, students will know that Jesus rose from the dead." The Resurrection is an important biblical and historical truth that young people should know; therefore, this is a good objective.

Keep in mind that lesson objectives should be measurable. You should be able to tell whether or not your meetings are successful, based on your objectives. A clear objective is important, not only because it keeps the activity in line with the overall purpose of the program, but also because it makes the rest of the planning process so much easier. The objective drives the event. It's like taking a trip in your car. If you know your destination is Indianapolis, you will travel on the roads that get you there.

You may think that all this talk about purposes, goals, and objectives sounds complicated and like a lot of busy work. It isn't. While it's true that at first this process may take some time, eventually it will become natural. In fact, before long, you will find yourself starting to ask "why" and "how" quite often. "Why are we doing this activity?" "How does this meeting help us reach our goals?" Whatever your role in the ministry, I urge you to take time to think through and write out your objectives.

After writing your objectives, you will be ready to plan the rest of the activity. A simple outline for a plan might look like this:

WHAT? (the specific activity)
WHERE?
WHEN?
WHO? (leaders and other ministry personnel)
HOW MUCH? (and who will pay the bills)

Remember that *Plan* comes *after Purpose* and *Philosophy*. Too many youth workers jump right into an activity or do something they enjoy doing, and then try to redirect the activity toward some unclear goal. The planning process requires much thought. Programs shouldn't be chosen "because we've always done it," because others are doing it, because they look good on paper, or for any reason other than the fact that they are in line with your philosophy and will accomplish your purpose.

PRINCIPLES

As you work through the *Purpose, Philosophy,* and *Plan* of your ministry, keep in mind the following principles.

1. *Be Realistic*
Beware of idealistic and unrealistic ministry goals and objectives. Remember that early adolescents have limited maturity, knowledge, and experience. Don't expect them to learn more or do more than they can handle.

God's in the Toybox

"Somehow, I think, in my lifetime our evangelical community has made the disastrous mistake of encouraging children to go beyond their depth in theological understanding; the result may be that doctrines introduced too soon and at too young an age are relegated to the closet of discarded toys later in life. Part of the reason for this may be that we've gotten away from the catechism and similar gradual, structured learning methods. Another part may be our fear lest a child shall not have made a 'decision' by age five or six.

"I'm not saying that no child can find reconciliation to God through faith at that young age; many can and do. But even for them, the nails of the cross, the crown of thorns, the deep things of our Christian faith may perhaps better wait for the development of conceptual thinking and experience in adolescence. If Jesus would receive the hardened criminal with the simple plea, 'Lord, remember me when You come into Your kingdom,' surely He will receive a little child with a simple understanding of Jesus' love.

"We're in such a hurry in contemporary America. And we're so inclined to interrupt or destroy childhood."

Joe Bayly, *Eternity Magazine*, January 1979.

The objective for a Sunday School lesson I read recently was to train students to share "The Romans Road" (a presentation of the Gospel using verses in Romans) with their friends. Besides the fact that this particular witnessing tool is geared toward adults, the goal is still unrealistic for early adolescents. Most junior highers don't realize (or even want to know) that their friends are lost and need Christ.

This is especially true of younger students. In grade school, most of their classmates were good kids. A few may have caused trouble, but nothing very serious. Most Christian children, then, assume that everyone is Christian (unless they are clearly Jewish, Hindu, Moslem, or Buddhist). And most Christian children have no real understanding of denominations. My fifth-grade daughter commented that Melissa must be Catholic because her parents were strict and wouldn't let her listen to rock music. Later I found out that Melissa went to a Bible church, and that her mom and dad were strong believers. Incidentally, my wife and I are more strict than they are.

Because junior highers haven't made clear Christian/non-Christian distinctions, a better objective would be that students learn that their friends need Christ. Then, another lesson could discuss the best way to reach them. Eventually the class could cover how to carefully and lovingly explain the plan of salvation.

Unrealistic goals for junior highers include expecting them to learn and understand the finer points of theology, to make a dramatic change in their families, to win their school for Christ, and to behave like adults. They may give the answers you want to hear or perform for you for a while, but eventually junior highers will act their age.

As youth leaders, it's also easy to get too optimistic about the results of our programs. For example, don't expect to have a hundred kids show up to a pizza party when your usual attendance is ten. And don't expect everyone to listen attentively to everything you say. Your young people will move around, talk, and make gross sounds—in other words, they will act like junior highers.

One night I was complaining to my wife about how the kids in

JV wouldn't invite other people to the meetings. She commented that inviting others, especially a whole bunch of others, was a new concept to this age-group. In all their activities so far, like Brownies, gymnastics, or soccer, kids signed up or joined. Gail suggested that instead of challenging kids to invite scores of acquaintances, I should encourage each of them to bring one or two of their close friends.

Of course, it's also possible to sell these young people short and to expect too little of them. For example, this age-group can be very service oriented. That's why they enjoy working in the church nursery and baby-sitting. This interest and potential for serving others can be channeled into some very meaningful projects in the church and community. Recognizing this, many churches now have special mission trips for these younger students.

Remember when you design your ministry to be realistic, keeping in mind the age and development level of the kids with whom you are working.

2. Be Relational
Jesus spent His entire public ministry training His twelve disciples. They walked, talked, ate, and ministered together. In effect, He poured His life into them. And throughout the Gospels we see Jesus entering into conversations, healing, loving, and reaching out and touching individuals. The core of Christ's ministry on earth was personal, building relationships with people and sharing Himself with them. In the same way, we should be relational in our ministry, following Christ's example.

We should also be relational because it is most effective. Books, magazines, television, radio, video, booklets, and large rallies can play a very important role in spreading the Good News. All are helpful tools. But the most effective ministry happens person-to-person. Think of how you came to Christ. Who introduced you to Him, and who has been most helpful in your growth in the faith? I remember godly parents, a sensitive pastor, Christian friends, a Sunday School teacher or two, and a caring youth minister. *People* make the difference, and no paper or program can take their place.

"Spiritual Dropouts"

"What is it about many current evangelistic methods that is so counterproductive to the goal?
1. A manipulative process tends to produce dropouts. This includes informative transmission (evangelism as a one-way communication of certain facts the hearer needs to know) and manipulative monologue (a sales pitch).
2. An evangelistic process that sees its goal as 'decisions' rather than 'disciple' tends to create dropouts.
3. An evangelistic process that presents the Gospel one time and then asks for a response tends to create dropouts.
4. An evangelistic process that does not build relationships with the local church, its programs, and its ministry tends to produce dropouts."

From "Closing the Evangelistic Back Door" by Win and Charles Arn, *Leadership Journal,* Spring 1984.

Junior highers are social animals. As mentioned in chapter 2, much of their time revolves around gaining and maintaining friendships. They need people who accept them as they are and care about them. And because they are changing in how they relate to their parents, they need adults who take time to listen to them and to tell them the truth. Be one of those adults for them. Make your ministry personal—be relational. (In chapter 6 we will examine more closely how to relate to junior highers at a personal level.)

3. *Be Responsible*
Irresponsible people don't care about what they do as long as they get results. And there are many irresponsible men and women in business, politics, and even the church who have left a trail of destruction in their wake as they have pushed, pulled, clawed, and climbed to the top.

Being a responsible minister to junior high young people means that you handle them with care, refusing to manipulate them for your own purposes, even if those purposes sound noble.

The visiting evangelist stood before the assembled Sunday School classes. Fifty pairs of eager and innocent childhood eyes gazed at him as he began to speak. Graphically he portrayed the wonders of heaven and the horrors of hell. And then he asked everyone to bow their heads and close their eyes. He paused for a moment and then broke the serious silence with a question. "How many of you want to stay out of hell?" He spat out "hell" with a snarl. "Raise your hands." Fifty hands shot up. "You can put them down," he continued. "And how many of you want to go to heaven?" The same fifty hands shot heavenward—it was unanimous. The evangelist concluded by leading the group in a prayer, assuring them that they had been saved. Then he left and recorded "50 decisions" on his personal statistics ledger.

That's manipulation, and it's irresponsible. The truth is that we could get most children and even early adolescents to do almost anything we wanted them to if we pushed the right emotional buttons. But that wouldn't be responsible, and it wouldn't be Christian. An overemphasis on competition can also be irresponsible. It's all right to reward kids, but don't get carried away. Being responsible means understanding where these young people are emotionally and handling them with care.

Because most junior highers are biblically illiterate (especially outside the church), much of our work will be pre-evangelism, laying the foundation and building a framework for the Gospel. We want young people to make real, solid, and life-changing decisions for Christ. We don't want them to respond out of peer pressure, emotional manipulation, or desire to please us. Remember whose needs you're meeting and be responsible in your ministry methods.

4. Be Real
I have three brothers, and we differ greatly. But we have one thing in common—we're all like Dad. Why? Besides genetics, it's due to the fact that he was our model of what it meant to be a man

and a father. I find myself repeating *his* encouragements and warnings with my children.

"Our children will follow our example, whether good or bad. They will adopt our values. The major moral decisions they make will be shaped by the values they learn from Mom and Dad. If we love cars, houses, clothes, money, or sports, so will they. If we love winning more than playing well, so will they. And if we follow God unreservedly, chances are they will too."

From *Kids in Sports* by Bill Perkins and Dr. Rod Cooper (Portland, Ore.: Multnomah Press, 1989).

We all model values, what is important to us. In fact, we cannot *not* model values. Values are communicated by how we act and react. Consider how you would react to a damaged book as compared to a dented car. You probably would get much more upset about the dented car. The car is worth more to you. That's a value. We also shout our values by how we spend our time, how we spend our money, and how we treat people.

Early adolescents need to see real Christians working out their real faith in real life. As mentioned earlier, these young people still look up to adults. We can have a powerful influence in their lives. They are watching us to see what values we demonstrate.

I still remember an experience I had at summer camp when I was a kid. We were playing "balloon stomp" in a field. That's the game where you tie a balloon to your ankle and then try to pop everyone else's balloon while protecting yours. Early in the game, our youth director's balloon was popped. Instead of dropping out, as the rules required, he continued to run around the field popping balloons. He was cheating. Whether he was just being immature or didn't want to lose, he made an impression. I'm sure he forgot that incident decades ago, but I never did, and I've found it difficult to respect him since then. He told us how *we* should live, but he couldn't do it.

Being real means living what we preach, and it means being vulnerable. It is important, therefore, for you to be open and honest with students about your struggles and successes in the Christian life. Let them see your love for your spouse and children; let them see your love for the church; and let them see your love for Christ.

5. *Be Relevant*
When discussing the development of early adolescents earlier, I mentioned that the focus of this age is on competence, achieving, being good at something. Your ministry should reflect this need. If you talk about "intimacy" (the emphasis of young adults) or about "identity" (the emphasis of late adolescents), your message will go right over their heads. Instead, you should minister where they are and teach them needed life skills.

"The peer group is influential today largely by default. Young people today as in the past need a 'bridge' to maturity, a smooth transition from childhood to adulthood. And in most cases, the only bridge available is the peer group.

"But teenagers today still desire acceptance and guidance from the adult community. They still need and want adult models whom they can imitate and emulate. They want someone they can look up to."

From "Every Kid Needs an Adult Friend" by Wayne Rice in *Parents and Children* (Wheaton, Ill.: Victor Books, 1986).

For many years I worked with high school students in Campus Life. Many of our discussions centered on topics like cliques, self-concept, sex and dating, future, family, loneliness, and so forth. The subjects were felt-need oriented, conceptual, and focused on identity. In junior high, however, the focus had to change because the kids were different. So we concentrated on teaching them life skills. (We will discuss the concept of life skills further in chapter 9.) Make relevance a priority as you minister to junior highers.

"There is a danger when the process and product are confused. Values cannot be demonstrated; they are modeled in everything said and done. Skills are not modeled; they are demonstrated and taught. One word of caution: You cannot choose which values to model—modeling conveys all the values you hold, both good and bad.

"Values are being eroded in our society. Recently Christians have emphasized the importance of modeling because we know that values must be conveyed to our young people in order for them to survive the world's temptations. Consider these questions:

● What values do you want modeled for your children?

● What values do you NOT want modeled for your children?

● What skills do you want your children to have?"

From "Can We Take Modeling Too Far?" by Dr. Bruce B. Barton and Dr. James C. Galvin in *Parents and Teenagers* (Wheaton, Ill.: Victor Books, 1984).

---

6. *Be Resourceful*

Hundreds of resources are available to you as a youth worker—use them. We are living in the age of technology and information—take advantage of that fact. More youth ministry tools are available now than ever before, so there's no excuse for having dull classes and boring meetings. (In the back of this book I've listed many of the books and other ministry tools currently available to youth workers.) And if you don't like the resources you've seen, write your own.

What I am suggesting is that you not *assume* anything when it comes to specific programs, activities, and events. Try something new. Do something "off the wall." Be creative. Who says your Sunday School class always has to meet in the same room with the chairs arranged in the same way? Who says your youth group always has to meet at the same time and place? Do whatever it takes, consistent with your philosophy of ministry, to achieve your purposes.

And try to catch kids by surprise. Our most popular events are "mystery meetings." We tell the kids to show up at church at a specific time, with a certain amount of money, and then we do something together. These aren't spectacular events, but they're special—and the kids love them. Last year, we went to a movie, to the mall, bowling, miniature golfing, on a treasure hunt, to a hockey game, and to a cemetery.

The sky's the limit for your ministry! Use your imagination and be resourceful.

7. Be Ready

Teachable moments are often unpredictable. We never know when we will have the opportunity to model a value, reinforce an important lesson, or point someone to Christ. And we can't schedule crises—those tragic and stressful times. Therefore, we must be ready, as Peter says, "to give an answer to everyone who asks you to give the reason for the hope that you have" (1 Peter 3:15).

Of course this means being available—we can't respond if we're not there. And it means being sensitive, listening carefully, and watching for signals.

Charlene answered a question in Sunday School with a shrug of her shoulders and a disgusted sigh. "We're supposed to love our parents. That's the answer." Obviously there was something behind her words. Later I discovered a serious conflict at home.

During a recent trip to a water park, a couple of the guys came to me complaining about how one of them had lost a ten dollar bill in the wave pool, another boy had found it, and the boy wouldn't give it back. After intervening, I discovered that the boy was friendly and quite willing to listen to reason. But I had to work hard to keep my kids from making this an angry confrontation and a test of egos. After we reached a solution, I was able to explain how their belligerent and argumentative attitudes had made the problem worse and how they could accomplish more by listening to the other person's side of the story.

Unfortunately there are other times when teachable moments have slipped right past me. Later, looking back, I have seen how I could have taken advantage of them—but I wasn't prepared. Be ready.

POSTLUDE

As vital as it is to minister to early adolescents, it is just as important to do it *right*. This means thinking through and designing your purpose, philosophy, and plan.

THINK IT THROUGH

1. List several possible purposes or goals of a youth ministry.

2. Which of these would be most appropriate for the youth with whom you will be working?

3. What are your ministry nonnegotiables? In other words, what principles would you include in your philosophy of ministry?

4. What young people have had the opportunity to spend concentrated amounts of time with you (at least an hour or two at a time)?

5. What are some of the values you communicated during those times?

6. What resources are available for you to use in your ministry?

CHAPTER 4

PARENTS: FRIENDS OR FOES?

I don't know when the desire was implanted. I certainly had no lifelong, overwhelming feeling or obsession. Maybe it was because Mom and Dad were such great role models or because family times held such good memories. Whatever my subconscious motivation, I just knew that I wanted to be a father someday. I looked forward to cuddling beautiful babies ("He has your eyes!"), marveling at her first toddling steps, teaching him how to throw and catch, watching and listening at the recitals with justifiable pride, and recording every important event on film.

As newlyweds, Gail and I talked about starting a family, and we agreed to wait a few years to give us time to establish our relationship. But we knew that when the time was right, God would give us children; and, of course, we would be terrific parents.

But it wasn't easy having children. In fact, it seemed almost impossible to conceive, even though we tried everything we could. Nothing seemed to work.

Then one day Gail had a miscarriage. Although disappointing, this showed us that pregnancy was possible (we didn't even know she was pregnant at the time), and we saw it as a step in the right direction. Then after more months of trying and hoping, Gail rushed home with the doctor's good news—she was pregnant again! A few weeks later, we felt confident enough to tell relatives and friends who rejoiced with us.

Only days after sharing the happy news, Gail walked into my office. I knew something was wrong—she should have been at school, and her eyes were red from crying. Then, rushing into my arms, she sobbed out those dreadful words: "The baby's dead. The baby's dead." Although I wanted to deny the test results from the hospital and the doctor's diagnosis, eventually I had to admit the truth. The fetus, our baby, had died, and we were back to square one in our efforts to become parents.

During the next few days and weeks, there were times when our grief seemed overwhelming. I remember crying out to God at night: "What's wrong? What have we done? Don't You trust us?" I knew of pregnant teenagers having conceived in the backseat of a car. And here we were, mature, Christian adults, dedicated to God's service—and we couldn't have children.

Eventually Gail became pregnant again. However, the pregnancy was very difficult. During those nine months, she had to be very careful—no traveling, no lifting, no pushing, and a lot of rest. In addition, Gail had a reaction to salt, a gall bladder attack, shingles, and, eventually, back labor. In the hospital, the doctor told me that Gail had acute toxemia. Later I learned that because of the poison in Gail's system, the baby had been losing weight, and both she and Gail could have died.

But on May 30, 1975, Kara burst into our lives. She was our five pounds of miracle, nestled in a pink blanket. Pain and problems forgotten, we marveled at our tiny, soft, innocent, and wrinkled gift from God—the most beautiful baby in the world!

Gail and I dreamed of what Kara would become. We had such plans and hopes! As Kara lay in Gail's arms in the hospital, we would talk about her and pray for her. And she never seemed to cry when she was with us.

"Welcome"

Daughter or son
Soon to be one
God's gift to our home

      The family tree
      Will then be three
      As you bid shalom

            Baby's a word
            Seldom's been heard
            Save in whispered prayers

            As miracle passed
            You came at last
            Transposing our cares

Tiny, soft, new
One made from two
As He did allow

      And so it seems
      All of our dreams
      Rest with you now

            Beginnings profound
            Potentials abound
            Alive from above

            Parents we're now
            But only know how
            To give you our love

Birth announcement poem written by Dave Veerman at the birth of Kara Beth, May 30, 1975.

At home, however, it was different. Kara had colic and wore us down and out with twenty-four hours of wailing interruptions. But even at 3 A.M., struggling to stay awake and get her back to sleep, I would pray about Kara's future and wonder what lay ahead. "Would she be musical, athletic, intelligent, beautiful?" And there was the almost overwhelming feeling of inadequacy. "I'm a rank amateur at parenting! How can Gail and I ever raise this fragile newborn into a woman of God?" I wondered between lullabies and prayers.

During those sleepless nights, I also learned about unselfish love and gained a new appreciation for my parents. I thought of what they must have done and felt at my birth—and how much of their love I had taken for granted over the years. I looked into Kara's tiny, innocent eyes and whispered, "You will never know, Kara, how much we love you, how much you mean to us, until you go through this yourself and have children of your own."

My adventure in parenting began there and has continued now into the teen years. Many of my pre-child, idealized dreams and ideas have materialized. But in the midst of moments of wonder, joy, and excitement, there have been questions, doubts, fears, disappointments, and struggles.

That's what it means to be a parent, not just for Gail and me but for all the parents I know. So much of us (probably too much) is wrapped up in our children—love, dreams, hope, and even identity. I would die for my girls, and I am very concerned about anything or anybody who would influence them.

That's why the key to junior high ministry is parents. You will have to work with and through them if you want to work with their children.

THEY CARE

I know there are abusive parents who harm their children emotionally and physically, and others who don't care what happens to their children. But I think that most parents *do* care and want only the best for their kids.

When I began working with high school students (in Campus Life) in the '60s, suspicious parents wondered if I was a Communist. In the '70s, especially in the wake of Jim Jones, the Moonies, and others, they questioned whether or not Campus Life was a cult. Then, in the '80s with stories of kidnappings and child pornography, they wondered if I was a pervert or some dirty old man. Although the suspicions changed over the years, the motives were the same—parents wanted to know who was working with their kids.

"There are four essential elements for a close family life. When present, they serve as a source of strength for adolescents. They are:
1. Parental harmony
2. Parent-youth communication
3. Parental discipline or control
4. Parental nurturing"

From *Five Cries of Parents* by Merton P. and A. Irene Strommen (San Francisco: Harper and Row, 1985).

At first, I was threatened by the questions and insinuations. But then I learned to thank those parents who called to find out more about me. Their calls showed that they cared. They also helped me realize that working with other people's children is a heavy responsibility.

HANDLE THEM WITH CARE

Early adolescents are still relatively young—just out of grade school—so most parents still see them as their "little boys and girls." Therefore, parents will tend to be much more protective of children at this age than when they are in high school, when they are driving and much more on their own.

Parents are most sensitive about the oldest child. Having read and heard about all the problems that young people face, they are fearful about what will happen to him or her and at the prospect of having a teenager in the house.

Communicate
Parents (especially good ones) want, and deserve, to know *who* is working with their son or daughter, *why* we are interested in him or her ("What's the ulterior motive?"), *what* we will be doing (and how they will be supervised), and *when* the activities begin and end. Safety heads the list of their concerns.

When I lived in Louisiana, every December during Christmas vacation, we would take a couple hundred high school students to Gatlinburg, Tennessee for Youth for Christ's "Winter Holiday." Our brochure was geared to kids, so it featured winter sports, great music, opportunities to meet new friends, and fun. But we also sent a letter to the parents of those who registered or expressed interest. In this letter we gave the daily schedule, explained who the counselors were and how many young people each one would be responsible for, described the transportation, outlined the rules and the possible punishments for breaking them, and even explained the emergency medical procedure. We wanted the parents to know that, although the trip would be fun, it would also be safe.

Anyone working with junior highers should communicate continually with parents. You can do this through letters, newsletters, phone calls, parents' meetings, and face-to-face encounters.

Relate
Of course the best way to head off a problem or diffuse any potentially explosive confrontation is to get to know a person and gain his or her confidence. This is especially important with parents. What you don't want is for them to ask and then answer their own questions. You should make yourself available to answer any questions that arise.

If you are young (e.g., a student, just out of college, or in your late twenties), let parents know that you don't have all the answers, but you love kids and want to help them. Assure parents that you are always open to their suggestions and will keep your conversations with them in confidence. If you are an older adult, especially a parent, you will be able to talk with parents as peers, sharing common experiences and discussing parenting ideas. In

"Just trying to decide when to hold on and when to let go is enough to drive any normal parent into a state of terminal stress. So maybe the solution is not to worry about it. Perhaps the answer is that simple. We just keep the relationship constant. Despite all her running around to avoid us at the concert, despite all her pleas for her own TV set so she won't have to be in the same room with us, despite all her plans for an 'unchaperoned' party at our house, we just keep going on about this business of being parents just as we always have. We won't panic. We won't yell. We won't even demand our rights or threaten her with independence since that is what she seems to want. We will just keep loving her and letting her know that we love her."

From *When Junior Highs Invade Your Home* by Dr. Cliff Schimmels (Old Tappan, N.J.: Fleming H. Revell Company, 1984).

either case, don't be afraid of parents. Treat them with respect and see them as allies.

ENLIST THEIR SUPPORT

High schoolers are much more independent than younger students, if for no other reason than the fact that they can drive. They don't have to depend on buses, parents, or car pools to take them to school and to various activities. Although Mom and Dad are nervous when Junior gets his driver's license, they appreciate not having to be the chauffeur, carting him and his friends all over town. High schoolers are also breaking away from home in other areas as their parents give them more freedom. When I worked with high school students, I could take them out for Cokes after school, arrange to meet them at various locations, and schedule activities at times that were best for them.

Consider the differences with junior high young people. First of all, they depend almost totally on their parents for transportation. Unless the place is close enough for them to walk or ride their bikes (during the day), someone, usually Mom or Dad, will have to drive them. This means that activities have to mesh with the family's schedule, not just the individual's. Parents are also concerned about their children having adequate rest and time for homework, so they protect their children's schedules. Remember, these are transition years for both parents and children.

My point is that parents are the gatekeepers. They have the responsibility and the power to control what their children do, all the way through junior high. And believe me, as a parent, it's easy to say no. Unless they know you and are sold on your program, they won't be of much help.

But this parental power can also be an advantage. If you gain parents' confidence and convince them that your program is just what their sons and daughters need, they will make sure their children attend. Whether it's Sunday School, youth group, Awana, Campus Life/JV, or a special event, sell the parents on it and the kids will be there.

This means that you will have to design your publicity on two levels. With the kids, emphasize the adventure, excitement, fun, and friends. With the parents, emphasize the content, values, relationships, and leadership. Let these mothers and fathers know that you are working with them to help their children grow mentally, socially, emotionally, and spiritually. Show them that you're on their side.

GET THEM ON YOUR TEAM

Parents can be a tremendous asset to your ministry. If possible, recruit parents to serve on the ministry team. (I will discuss this further in chapter 5.) Remember, at this age, young people are quite open to adults—even their parents. Some people think that kids don't like having their parents in meetings or at activities. That may be the case in certain situations, but I have found the opposite to be true. In fact, having Mom or Dad involved tends to enhance the relationship between parent and child. (If you're in doubt, ask the young person about it.)

"It seems to me that if youth ministry is to continue to thrive, we need to be doing more and more with parents.

"I have three parents on my volunteer team. Best move I ever made!"

Greg Lafferty, Junior High Minister of the Wheaton Bible Church (Wheaton, Illinois).

Here are a few of the strengths that parents can bring to your ministry.

1. *Automatic access to the school—the building, the administrator, and the faculty*

In the role of professional youth worker, I had to continually win the right to go on campus, even in schools where I had served for thirteen years. Although I had a great relationship with the administration and faculty and had worked closely with them, still I was an outsider. One false move, and I could be out on my ear. When I began to work with Campus Life/JV in my community, I couldn't believe the difference that being a parent made. When I walked through the doors of the middle school and into the office, I was Kara's father and received royal treatment. Everyone was polite and friendly, listening carefully and trying to assist me.

School administrators are very sensitive to parents because the parents' children are in that building. When I spoke with the assistant principal about the JV program and told her that it was sponsored by a parent committee, she thanked me for what we were doing and offered the school facilities for our use. I was doing virtually the same thing that I had done in the high school ministry, but here they welcomed me.

A good relationship with school administrators is important for anyone who wants to have a personal ministry with young people. Sunday School teachers and others will have occasion to visit schools to pick up kids, talk with counselors, attend events, and so forth. And remember, parents are always permitted to be at school.

2. *Natural contact with students*

As a young Campus Life staff member, I had to schedule my time carefully to be with students. This involved going on campus, watching practices, and attending school events. We called this "contacting" and "building time." Because relationship building requires time, I worked hard to be with kids.

Today, as a parent, I am amazed at how much contacting takes place in the course of a week without even trying. Yesterday, I drove five girls to school; last weekend, a couple of others were at the house; Gail and I were chaperones for the school's activity night; I go to most of Kara's volleyball and basketball games; and I see tons of kids when I jog through the neighborhood. Being with kids used to be part of my job—now it's part of my life.

Again, this contact is important for any kind of youth ministry. Even if you are only working with a small group of students at church, your involvement with them in the neighborhood and with their friends will help reinforce the values you represent, will encourage the young people to live for Christ, and will help them reach out to friends.

3. *Credibility with other parents*

When parents learn that other parents are sponsoring and running a youth activity or program, they are much more willing to allow their children to become involved. I find this true both with Campus Life/JV and our church youth group. I'm not someone they have to get to know. I live in the white house on the corner, near the grade school; I'm Kara and Dana's dad; and we've seen each other at swim meets, PTA meetings, block parties, school activities, and other community events. I'm not a stranger—they know me. And I'm working at parenting just as they are.

4. *Knowledge about kids*

All parents are amateurs—no one is an expert on how to raise his or her child. But all parents know much about young people from personal experience.

Because I have a teenager living in my house, I am constantly involved in a real life, youth ministry laboratory. I am learning firsthand what adolescents are like and how to relate to them. Of course, I am also learning how much I do *not* know, so I welcome the advice and help of youth ministers and other parents.

GET THEM INVOLVED

Of course not all parents should be on the ministry team. Some parents may not be Christians, may not be interested, or may not have the ability. Even so, working with parents will provide other resources and opportunities.

1. *They will volunteer their time*

Most parents of younger children are used to being asked to work as volunteer coaches, room mothers, swim meet timers, and other assorted roles for just about every activity in which their kids have become involved. And, as mentioned above, they drive their children everywhere. Most parents volunteer to help in some way, even if it's just to coordinate transportation.

When I signed up my daughters for soccer, a line on the form read, "Where would you like to help?" and then it listed various options. Note that it did not ask, "Would you like to help?"

This doesn't mean that parents have a lot of free hours to donate. But they expect to be asked to help out—and usually will. Some have more time than others. Single parents, for example, will be much more limited, but still they will do what they can. Parents often approach me both at church and in the neighborhood and ask how they can help with my ministry.

2. *They will provide services*

Besides time, most parents will gladly take their turn hosting meetings, bringing refreshments, driving, typing, making phone calls, and so forth. They know that these tasks are necessary and that they should do their part.

3. *They will give spiritual and moral support*

Christian parents are well aware of the spiritual needs of their young person and his or her friends. Recently I told our associate pastor that, as a parent of a teenager and an almost-teen, I ache for other Christian adults to be involved in my daughters' lives. I want them to have positive role models and to hear our values affirmed from others whom they admire and trust.

"It is a fact that most parents have a feeling of love toward their children. It is assumed, however, that parents naturally convey this love to a child. This is the greatest error today. Most parents are not transmitting their own heartfelt love to their children, and the reason is that they do not know how. Consequently, many children today do not feel genuinely, unconditionally loved and accepted.

"This, I feel is the case in most children's problems today. Unless parents have a basic love-bond relationship with their child, everything else (discipline, peer relationships, school performance) is on a faulty foundation, and problems will result."

From *How to Really Love Your Child* by Dr. Ross Campbell (Wheaton, Ill.: Victor Books, 1977).

If we challenge Christian parents to pray, they will; and they will enlist others to join the prayer team. In organizing a new Campus Life/JV ministry in a neighborhood, our first step was to have a meeting of Christian parents. At this meeting, we didn't recruit to fill any of the volunteer positions on the ministry team. Instead we explained the ministry and challenged the parents to pray for the junior highers they knew in their homes, neighborhoods, and churches. We felt that if all we did was motivate and mobilize parents to prayer, the meetings would be successful. Imagine the impact on your church if parents and others would pray regularly for the young people in the congregation and for your ministry with them.

Parents will also encourage us. They appreciate the fact that someone cares about their children. During the last couple of years, at three neighborhood parties, a father has said essentially the same thing to me on each occasion: "That's a really good thing you're doing with that JV program. Thanks." He's not from an evangelical church and doesn't know all the subtleties of the ministry, but he knows what it means to his daughter—and he's thankful.

4. *They will give financial support*
As mentioned earlier, junior high parents are critically aware of the need for responsible ministry to adolescents. They see the need in their own homes as their junior highers grow up before their eyes. Therefore, they understand the ministry and are willing to support it—especially if they are involved personally as a member of the ministry team or as a pray-er, driver, or refreshment provider.

One of my neighbors handed me $25, explaining that she wanted to help with our expenses. Two fathers donated $150 to buy *Campus Life* magazine subscriptions for the graduating eighth-graders. One of the easiest budget items to gain approval in our church is junior high ministry. Parents will help financially because they know the need for and see the results of the ministry.

5. *They will be open to the Gospel*
As children enter early adolescence, parents become very sensitive to their own inadequacies and very open to suggestions and support. This is true for *all* parents, not just those in the Christian community. A junior higher could be the bridge for establishing relationships with these concerned or even hurting parents and eventually introducing them to Christ. You could have a parents' meeting; sponsor a parenting seminar; tell them about Focus on the Family, The Gathering of Men, and other adult ministries; give copies of *Parents and Teenagers,* the *Life Application Bible,* and other resources; or invite them to church. As they get to know you and you discuss their children, they will begin to trust you and be receptive to your loving witness.

Although parents can seem like "the enemy," questioning our motives and analyzing our moves, we must realize that parents

"A mother once wrote to me for advice, having reached the end of her rope over the entertainment issue with her teenage daughter. Perhaps her cry for help sounds all too familiar:

'I have been knocking heads with my 13-year-old daughter over the music issue. She resents me telling her which rock albums I will allow her to buy and listen to. I'm not her favorite person these days anyway, and I am afraid this issue is becoming a giant wedge in our relationship. What can I do?' "

From "Teen Tune-Up: A Parent's Primer on Popular Youth Culture" by Robert DeMoss, Jr. (Pomona, Calif.: Focus on the Family, 1989).

and youth workers are really on the same side. Working with parents is the key to successful junior high ministry. Instead of fearing and avoiding parents, we should get to know them, communicate with them, get them involved in the program, and minister to them.

Working with junior high young people offers you a rare opportunity to impact whole families for Christ because of the concern and commitment of parents. Don't miss it!

THINK IT THROUGH

1. Imagine that you are the parent of a young person about to enter junior high or middle school. What would be some of your concerns and worries?

2. What might you think if your son or daughter came home from school and told you about an adult who was hanging around talking with kids?

3. As a youth minister (volunteer or professional), what would you say to describe your ministry to a non-Christian parent? To a Christian parent?

4. For what tasks or ministry team roles do you think you could recruit parents?

5. List Christian parents who would be good candidates for serving on the ministry team.

6. List parents of junior highers who might be open to ministry in their own lives.

7. What could you do to minister to those parents?

CHAPTER 5

BUILDING THE TEAM

Everyone is in place and set. Looking over the defense, the quarterback barks out his verbal code. The wide receiver goes in motion from right to left, shadowed by a defender in the defensive backfield. Suddenly bodies explode across the neutral zone, each man thrusting hundreds of pounds of muscle forward, trying to move and control his opponent. The left tackle blocks to the right, double-teaming the defensive lineman with the left guard. Pulling left, down the offensive line, the right guard hits the defensive tackle, pushing him out. At that precise moment, the quarterback, having faked a pitchout, hands the ball to the tailback who follows the fullback through the hole. The linebacker moves to fill but is hit by the charging fullback. Cutting to the right off that block, the ball carrier is finally tackled by a defensive back after a nine-yard gain.

Football is a team sport. Although the quarterback, tailback, and wide receivers get most of the credit for the offense, the success of each play depends on eleven athletes carrying out their assignments. Knowing this, the wise coach carefully selects team players whose abilities and strengths complement each other and then molds them into an efficient and effective unit.

Teamwork is also important in youth ministry. Of course it is possible to reach young people by yourself, building relationships and sharing Christ with individuals, but you will be much more effective if you build a ministry team. Remember, even the Lone Ranger had Tonto.

THE VALUE

The genius of any team is that the whole equals more than the sum of the parts. If I am working alone, I can accomplish a certain amount. If you help me, we can accomplish more than just double my work, especially if your abilities compliment mine. Our planning, thinking, talking, and lifting should increase our productivity more than twofold. Certain tasks in life may be best accomplished by the individual, but youth ministry is not one of them. The task is too great, the stakes are too high, and the message is too vital. And consider the following advantages offered by a team approach.

1. *Uses Gifts*

Romans 12:5-6 says, "So in Christ we who are many form one body, and each member belongs to all the others. We have different gifts, according to the grace given us."

Each individual Christian has a unique blend of natural abilities, developed talents, and spiritual gifts. God can use each person's strengths to build up the body of Christ and to reach others for Him. I know of no one who has every spiritual gift—not even full-time Christian workers. One person may be a musician; another may be a great administrator; and someone else may be an excellent teacher. With a team approach, one person's strength can compensate for another's weakness.

2. *Eases Workload*

Youth ministry involves much time and effort, and even the most dedicated and talented individual will become exhausted trying to carry the load by himself or herself.

Fresh out of college and into full-time youth work, I was assigned three high schools to reach for Christ. Each of these schools had over 3,000 students, so my mission field numbered nearly 10,000. Needless to say, I felt overwhelmed. Your assignment may not be so broad, but still it is large. Even with a handful of young people, there are classes and events to plan, calls to make, parents to meet, school activities to attend and, of course, kids to relate to, challenge, and counsel.

The wisest man on earth wrote: "Two are better than one, because they have a good return for their work: If one falls down, his friend can help him up. But pity the man who falls and has no one to help him up! Also, if two lie down together, they will keep warm. But how can one keep warm alone? Though one may be overpowered, two can defend themselves. A cord of three strands is not quickly broken" (Ecclesiastes 4:9-12). Team members can share the load.

3. Offers Variety

Having more than one person involved adds variety to a ministry. It's helpful for young people to see Christ at work in many lives and to hear the message from more than one source. On a personal level, not everyone relates to the same kind of individual. And because of where junior highers are socially and the special needs of each sex, it is best if women work with the girls and men with the boys.

This approach also gives team members variety. One person may help teach Sunday School for a quarter; then she might work with the youth group for the next few months. Altering assignments keeps a ministry fresh and gives leaders the chance to see kids in different settings.

4. Supplies Replacements

In the course of a year, situations arise that prevent people from carrying out their assignments — emergencies, sicknesses, vacations, and so forth. When these inevitable interruptions arise, other team members can fill in and carry on the ministry. That's one reason why two couples on our ministry team are in charge of Sunday School and another three or four people work with the youth group. Gail and I assist Dick and Debbie Simmers with the youth group. When Dick was called out of town on business, I led the meeting. Team members cover for each other.

We also live in a very transient area. Many of our church members are transferred every three years, so our turnover rate for church responsibilities is very high. Having a ministry team protects us from leadership gaps and insures continuity.

Who Volunteers and Why

- About 45% of adults 18 years of age or older reported volunteering in 1987.
- Time given to volunteer work averaged 4.7 hours a week.
- People 65–74 volunteered the most (6 hours a week), followed by those 45–54 (5.8 hours).
- People with household incomes of $20,000 to $30,000 volunteered most often, followed by those earning $50,000 to $75,000.
- People volunteered to do something useful (56%), because they would enjoy the work (34%), because a family member or friend would benefit (27%), or for religious reasons (22%).

From *Newsweek* magazine, July 10, 1989. Based on a 1988 survey for independent sector conducted by the Gallup organization.

---

5. *Provides Support*
Never forget that youth ministry is a battle—not with kids or parents (although it may seem that way at times), but with Satan. (Check out Ephesians 6:12.) In an effort to capture these young lives, he will throw obstacles and opposition at us to cause us to

become discouraged with our ministry and give up. As Ron Hutchcraft says, it's a battle for a generation. That's why we need prayer and encouragement. In fact, our first priority should be to enlist a group of men and women who will pray for the junior highers, for us, and for the ministry. Because members of the ministry team know they are in the battle together, they support each other.

SELECTION

Most churches have more jobs than workers and more assignments than volunteers, so those in charge of a ministry area often recruit any available person to fill a vacancy. Some people volunteer because they feel guilty ("Well, I suppose I should—I haven't taken my turn yet"); others because they're naive; and some because they can't say no. As a result, positions are filled by many who are uncalled, unmotivated, and unqualified—from serving on boards to teaching Sunday School.

Don't let that happen with the junior high ministry team. Instead, after informing the church of the needs and responsibilities of the ministry and challenging people to respond, choose carefully those you would have serve.

There are three basic criteria to use when "recruiting" and selecting the ministry team.

1. *Spirituality*

Although it's not necessary to have a team of spiritual giants, those who minister to young people should have a maturing and growing faith in Christ. In other words, they should be solid Christians who live what they profess and teach. Early adolescents are impressionable, and they watch us closely. We want them to see solid Christian values in our lives.

I once had a staff member who was kicked out of a restaurant for being rowdy and abusive to a waitress. I'm sure the kids with him thought it was funny, but think of what they were learning about how to treat others and being an adult. And I could write another book about the young lives that have been devastated by the marital problems or moral failings of their leaders.

On-the-Job Training

A simple four-step formula can be used when full-time staff train volunteers, and also when volunteers train other volunteers:
1. Explain the skill.
2. Demonstrate the skill.
3. Ask the person to explain the skill to you.
4. Supervise the person as he/she practices the skill.
    Step three is a simple check for understanding. The feedback in step four helps the trainer know whether or not the person is on the right track.

You can't know everyone's heart, nor can you guarantee anyone's spiritual success, but do your best to choose those who have a solid relationship with Christ.

2. *Motivation*
My parents' generation used the word "burdened" to describe a personal sense of God's calling someone to a specific ministry. And I can think of no better word to use here. Look for those who are burdened for junior high young people. You can hear the burden in their conversation and in their prayers. They are concerned for this age-group and want to reach them for Christ. Of course it may be hard to find burdened volunteers in this age of materialism and consumerism.

In Youth for Christ, our strategy for building a ministry team was to begin by identifying Christian parents of junior highers in a particular school district. Then, at a meeting with them, we would tell them about the need for the ministry and the structure of Campus Life/JV. We would also challenge them to pray for the junior highers they knew and for their possible roles in the ministry. These parent meetings were *not* sales pitches designed to recruit team members. But in the discussions that followed, those who were burdened for young people quickly surfaced. We challenged *those* parents to be on the team.

And that's why parents make such ideal team members. They are eyewitnesses to the need, and they care. Adults of any age can work with junior highers. Early adolescents have not yet turned off the older generation. In fact, most junior highers still respect and listen to their elders.

Your team could also include college students and even high schoolers. Junior highers almost idolize them. Older kids can have a great impact. Be sure, however, to use the *same selection criteria* for these students as you use with adults. They should be committed Christians, motivated to minister to this age-group. Remember, you want them to be positive role models. Don't use the junior high ministry to keep older kids involved or as a way to force them to grow up.

3. *Talents/Gifts*
This criterion is the least important of the three because the quality of the person is much more significant than his or her abilities. We should consider, however, the strengths that each person brings to the team. Some are good administrators, but have trouble relating to young people on a personal level. Others, filled with enthusiasm and creativity, are terrific at running games and activities. Some may be good at leading and managing. And there are those who are gifted teachers.

To some extent, the people on the team will determine the specific areas of responsibility. But it also works the other way. In other words, your purpose, philosophy, and plan may help you decide the team's configuration.

STRUCTURE
As you build the ministry team, it will be helpful to outline what is expected from each team member.

1. *Time*
"Super volunteers" exist who will put in 10–15 hours a week in youth ministry. Their commitment and energy are commendable, but they are the exceptions. (Usually they are young and single.)

One-on-One Review

The one-on-one review is a 30-minute meeting in which you discuss with a volunteer how his or her ministry with the students is going. This five-step outline is very helpful for knowing how to conduct the review.
1. Ask how the person is doing.
2. Read his or her ministry reports and give feedback.
3. Discuss problems and goals.
4. Develop an action plan.
5. Share prayer requests and pray together.

Most people don't have that kind of time to give to the ministry and will say no to your request.

Three hours a week is much more realistic. This may not seem like much, but it will work if you have enough people and limit the scope of each responsibility. For example, if leading the youth group involves planning, publicizing, and running all the weekly meetings, it will take much more than three hours a week. But if you divide those responsibilities among two or three people, each job can be managed. Another possibility is having the youth group meet every other week. This would also decrease the amount of time needed from each leader.

I am an active volunteer in my church and community. I chair the grade school carnival, sing in the church choir, help with worship, occasionally teach adult Sunday School, and work with the Gathering of Men in addition to my junior high ministry involvements. Obviously the total amount of time required for these responsibilities is more than ten hours a week. If any one of them demanded that kind of time commitment, I would have refused. But because they came in three hour increments (or less), I knew I could manage them—so I said yes, one request at a time.

The quality and commitment of volunteers does not diminish with the decrease in the time required. You can get a great volunteer for three hours a week.

2. *Roles*

To determine the ministry roles, think through everything that has to be done. Then see if you can divide the responsibilities to match the interests and abilities of your team members. For the junior high ministry at church, we have two couples in charge of Sunday School and three people in charge of the youth group. In addition, one woman serves as our secretary, lining up homes for meetings, putting announcements in the church bulletin, and sending out schedules. My role is to lead the team, help with the youth group, and plan the mystery meetings.

Here are the recommended volunteer positions and their descriptions for Campus Life/JV. Note that each one describes the task and the kind of person needed.

"One of the most frustrating volunteer problems youth workers encounter is that junior high ministry attracts adults, of any age, who are actually kids. Some adults haven't completed their adolescence and are attracted by the lifestyle and antics of young teenagers. These adults are looking for acceptance and, to some degree are continuing to try out new identity patterns themselves.

"While many youth workers enjoy being a bit juvenile at times (otherwise we probably wouldn't be interested ourselves in junior high ministry), it's important to find adults who enjoy being adults."

From "Shopping for Jr. High Volunteers" by Scott Noon, *Group's Junior High Ministry*, September/October 1989.

● TEAM LEADER—recruits and supervises the other team members, runs staff meetings, and may substitute if someone is gone. This person needs management and supervision skills.
● MC/PROGRAM COORDINATOR—leads the weekly meetings with the teacher and runs the games. This person needs up-front skills.

● TEACHER—leads the weekly meetings with the MC and presents the life skills each week. This person needs teaching skills.

● PERSONAL MINISTRY COORDINATOR—matches young people with staff for counseling and ensures that follow-through is taking place. This person needs personal ministry skills.

● TRANSPORTATION COORDINATOR—enlists parents and others to drive kids to the weekly meetings and other events and lines up buses, vans, etc. when needed. This person needs organizing skills.

● SPONSORING SCHOOLTEACHER—represents the ministry on campus, serving as a liason with administration and faculty and communicating with students through school announcements, etc. This person needs to work at the school.

Some groups have added other responsibilities, including secretary, refreshment coordinator, fund-raiser, substitute teacher, and others. You can divide the ministry almost any way you wish. Use your imagination.

A church in my community has a large junior high Sunday School department, so they have broken the large group down into small groups of 6–8 kids, each with an adult leader. Another church found that for large events they needed a technical staff, team leaders and assistants, crowd controllers, and a clean-up crew in addition to the regular ministry staff.

Most junior high groups are small. Regardless of size, the ministry should be divided into manageable units with responsibilities well defined. The positions on your ministry team should be determined by the structure of the program and the people available.

SUPERVISION

Whether you are a professional youth worker or a volunteer team leader, much of the success of the ministry team will depend on how well you supervise them. Just remember these four words beginning with "T," and you'll do all right.

● Team—Make sure that everyone knows it's a team effort. You're all in it together. This means having staff meetings in which you fellowship, plan, troubleshoot, and pray.

• *Time*—There's no substitute for relationships, but relationships take time. Get to know your team, and let them know that you are available to talk and pray. Communicate regularly through meetings, phone calls, letters, newsletters, and personal conversations. A good relationship will also win you the right to be heard when you have to confront someone about a problem.

• *Training*—Volunteers often feel unqualified and even intimidated by the ministry. Be constantly on the lookout for books, videos, and other resources that you can pass along to the team. Share your expertise with them; and, if the budget allows, send them to special seminars on youth work. Check the back of this book for a list of resources.

• *Thanks*—No matter how dedicated and committed they are, no one wants to be taken for granted. Let team members know that you appreciate them. Express your gratitude with a year-end dinner; books or other gifts; recognition in the bulletin, church newsletter, and worship service; or just sincere thank-you notes. People need to know that they are valued. You can never say "thanks" too often.

Volunteers need this kind of attention—and they deserve it.

Although it is far from being a game, youth ministry is a team sport. There are no stars on the team, just men and women who care about kids and use their gifts and abilities to reach them for Christ. Build the team with care and prayer.

THINK IT THROUGH

1. What volunteer responsibilities do you now have? Which one do you enjoy the most? Why?

2. Who recruited you to take that position? What convinced you to do so?

3. List the possible roles your junior high ministry team could have.

4. List the people you know who would meet the criteria (spirituality, motivation, talents/gifts) and could be possible ministry team members.

5. To what youth ministry training resources do you have access?

6. What could you do to motivate and mobilize people in your church or community to pray for junior highers and the ministry?

CHAPTER 6

GETTING CLOSE

Thus far we've discussed what early adolescents are like,
the need for working with this age-group, how to get
organized, the role of parents, and how to build a ministry
team. Now we come to the heart of the matter, relating to
junior highers themselves.

In the second chapter, I said that ministry should be
"relational." In other words, the most responsible and
most effective way to reach young people is through
getting to know them and building relationships
with them.

This principle is not limited to youth work or even to
ministry. Every day I receive a number of sales calls —
through the mail, on the phone, or even at my door.
Almost always I toss the letter or say I'm not interested,
before even hearing the pitch. But if a friend of mine
writes, calls, or stops by and wants to tell me about his
exciting new product or service, I will hear him out. The
relationship makes the difference. My friend has
won the right to be heard.

Consider your spiritual journey. How were you won to Christ? Who has influenced you the most? Probably a person who cared. Other means of communication have their place as valuable tools. Broadcast and print media, for example, can support and reinforce the spread of the Gospel. But the message must be personalized, carried, and communicated by a person—a friend—someone known and respected.

You can design the sharpest brochures, sponsor the wildest activities, host the most creative and exciting meetings, and even serve the tastiest refreshments—and you may attract large crowds. But without love, your efforts will be hollow. (That's my paraphrase of 1 Corinthians 13:1.) If your purpose is changing lives, you must build relationships.

AN OUTDOOR EDUCATION

One May afternoon, Kara burst into the kitchen after school and breathlessly announced, "There's outdoor education coming up, and they need parents to come—so do you want to help?" Then, placing her book bag on the table, she reached in and pulled out a note from the school with the details. "Outdoor Education" was an annual overnight experience for fifth-graders at a camp in Wisconsin (about an hour and a half away). The schedule would include nature walks, initiative tests, group-building exercises, and games. And because the two grade schools involved feed into the junior high these students would attend next year, it would be a good opportunity for them to get to know kids from the other school. Parent volunteers were needed to serve as overnight chaperones.

As a youth ministry veteran, I was used to camps, camping, kids, and counselors, so I volunteered. "So what if I lose a little sleep," I thought. "This will be a good opportunity to get to know these kids." I was confident in my ability to relate, have fun, and keep control.

When I arrived at the camp, just after dinner, I was assigned a cabin. There were two sides to this cabin, joined by a common bathroom, and a counselors' room. Boys from Brookdale Elementary (my school) were on one side, and boys from Longwood Elementary were on the other. My fellow counselor was a Longwood father and junior high teacher.

Around 8:30, everyone was told to head for the cabins. "Lights out" was 9:30. Gathering our group in one room, we introduced ourselves and read the rules. Then I pulled out a couple of games that I knew they would enjoy. These crowdbreakers had worked great with high schoolers.

But no one was interested. Instead, they wanted to play cards and throw things at each other, so I retreated from plan A and decided just to control the chaos.

Around 9:15, I got their attention and explained what I expected of them. I tried the "good guy, friendly, reasonable" approach that had worked on some high school retreats. I said that although I would turn the lights off at 9:30, I didn't care when they actually went to sleep as long as they were quiet and didn't keep anyone else awake. I smiled and tried to appeal to their good will and good sense. They all seemed to understand, so after everyone was in bed, I turned out the lights and went to my room.

The place erupted! In fact, every time I left them, they went wild. Obviously the friendly approach wasn't working.

Then, during one of the brief interludes when I had gotten them relatively quiet, I went to the other room. My fellow counselor was seated in front, like a prison guard, watching his group carefully. Anyone who disobeyed had to do a prescribed number of push-ups.

About that time I heard more noise from the guys on my side of the cabin. I was desperate, so I thought I would try my partner's approach. I pulled up a chair, acted as stern and tough as I could, and meted out punishments to fit the crimes—the prescribed push-ups and so forth. What I couldn't believe is that the guys actually did what I told them. Think about it. I had no real authority to back up my words—I wasn't a teacher, principal, or coach. I was just a volunteer trying to keep the peace. And yet they obeyed.

Eventually, things quieted down and everyone went to sleep. As I lay in my bunk, I thought about how those boys probably saw me as a mean person, a bad guy. I felt sorry for Kara, because I knew they would tell her how terrible her father was.

But the next morning, they were friendly. We laughed together in the breakfast line. And the worst offender the night before told Kara, "Your dad is really cool!" I couldn't believe my ears. I had done nothing "cool." I hadn't even tried being funny and had given

---

Ministering to Junior High Girls

Foundation 1: Have an awareness of the differences between boys and girls.
Foundation 2: Realize the special needs of this age-group of girls.
Foundation 3: Design a strategy to meet those needs.

Differences	Needs	Strategy
Physical: • Develop ahead of boys • Concerned about appearance	• To accept the changes	• Activities that don't change appearance • Nonathletic event can be boys vs. girls; otherwise mix teams
Social: • More serious conversation • Big group oriented • Aggressively pursue boys • Verbal distractors	• To talk • To be part of group • To develop relational competency • To express self verbally (boys distract physically)	• Balance activities with discussion time • Don't single them out • Reinforce appropriate behavior • Use peer pressure for discipline
Mental: • Grasp concepts more quickly	• To be challenged	• Explore possibility of outside input
Emotional: • Life is "tragic" • Emotional ups and downs	• To gain perspective on personal situations • To understand that the changes are normal	• Develop simple action plans for situational problems • Meetings should take into account these ups and downs

By Laura Laffoon and Carla Waterman of Youth for Christ.

up being nice. I had just been a policeman, but this young man thought that was cool.

That experience was an outdoor education for *me*. And I began to learn how to relate to this age-group.

HOW TO RELATE

Encourage every member of your ministry team to begin to relate on a personal level with the young people in your group. Some team members may only get to know one or two young people, but that will help. Here are some basic principles for relating to junior highers.

1. *Be Adult*

In my work with high school students, it took time to break down personal barriers and to build confidence with kids. Eventually they were comfortable enough to begin calling me "Dave." They knew I was an adult, but they felt free to be personal, so they called me by my first name. I related to them, especially the older ones, almost as peers. We talked about issues in the world and in their lives, thought through great concepts and ideas, and discussed the claims of Christ. But I probably couldn't have done that with junior highers. Early adolescents are different and need to be treated differently.

Junior highers still have a high degree of respect for adults and their authority. The boys in my cabin were ready to accept me because I was Kara's dad and because I represented the school. And after spending just a short time with them, they even liked me. There weren't the same barriers that I had found in high school ministry.

I must also add that I've never enjoyed the same "closeness" with junior highers that I have with high schoolers, even those who have been in the program for two or three years. Although we've spent many hours together, they still relate to me as an adult. And they call me "Mr. Veerman." But that distance or formality doesn't hinder communication. They'll never be my "buddies," but we can be friends.

Building friendships with junior highers does not involve stripping yourself of your adulthood and somehow taking on the disguise of a kid, dressing a certain way and using current slang expressions. It does mean taking time to understand these young people—their ways of thinking, their language, and their struggles. Junior highers haven't yet turned off the older generation—be an adult.

2. Be Assertive

Relationships with early adolescents must happen within structure. This means establishing limits and exercising discipline (which we'll discuss further in chapter 11). As I discovered at the camp, enforcing the rules did not diminish my standing with those boys (my fellow counselor, the junior high teacher, knew that). In fact, the opposite seemed to be true—being firm and even stern enhanced the relationships.

Good parents know that they have to set rules and enforce them. It would be irresponsible to allow children to do anything they felt like doing. Good junior high teachers know this, and they insist on conformity in the classroom and halls. Early adolescents need structure. Left on their own, without limits or enforcement, many go wild (as I experienced at Outdoor Education with my first attempt at maintaining order). Regardless of what they might say at the moment, I think that subconsciously they know that rules protect them from themselves, and that left on their own they would self-destruct. You can't love junior highers without disciplining them.

This means setting boundaries for your activities and meetings, stating clearly the rules and the consequences for breaking them, and enforcing those rules and carrying out necessary punishments. Be clear, fair, and firm.

Discipline, limits, and rules will only hurt a relationship if they are inconsistent or unfair or enforced in anger. Let the individual know that you still accept and affirm *him*, but that his *behavior* is unacceptable. Then make him endure the consequences of his actions.

Don't let your young people walk all over you. Be assertive, and set limits. Kids will respect you for it.

3. Be Available
In a world of instant coffee, microwave dinners, immediate answers, and simple solutions, it's easy to think that *anything* can happen quickly, almost instantaneously, if we only have the right formula. Unfortunately, such is not the case. Relationships don't happen quickly. They develop slowly, over time. Not that you have to be with someone *constantly* to become a friend, but you have to spend some time together and then be nearby or at least available.

Somebody has to be there
When the crowds have scattered
And the speaker
Has rushed away to catch a plane
To another city.
To another crowd.
Somebody has to be there
To pick up the ones who are left.
The ones who are strangers
The misfits. Square pegs
Being shoved by a sensible world
Into round holes.
Somebody has to be there
To comfort the awkward ones
Who have been loved
To death on Sunday
And left to die on Monday
While the personalities
Flit about in a circle
Of acceptance,
Never guessing at the loneliness
Of strangers.

by Lydia I. Carlson
Naperville, Illinois

Todd is my neighbor. I've known him for about five years. Last year he began sixth grade and started coming to our junior high club. Todd and I have a good relationship, not because we have done so much together, but because he has known me for a while. I am in his world, and I am available to him. Craig, however, lives on the other side of the subdivision. I've seen him at school and in the neighborhood riding his bike. He has also come to JV a couple of times. Our relationship is beginning to develop because Craig knows who I am, sees me often, and knows that I care about him.

Spending time with junior high kids means attending the choir concert, watching volleyball practice, shooting baskets with a few of them at the park, or taking a group of them out for pizza after the game.

This is another area where junior highers differ greatly from older youth. When I worked with high schoolers, I would often take a guy out for a Coke to talk things over. Junior highers don't respond as well to the individual approach. In fact, they may feel quite uncomfortable one-on-one, not knowing what to talk about. It would be better to spend time with a small group of friends. There will be opportunities for talking individually with these young people, but the relationship-building will be more effective at activities or with small groups.

Don't think you can walk into a group and immediately have their friendship. Schedule time to be with kids, getting to know them and letting them know you.

4. Be Active

The best way to get to know junior highers is through activities, by doing things together. Go out for ice cream, ride bikes, go shopping, take in a ball game, play Nintendo, watch a movie—the list is almost endless. Junior highers are filled with energy, they want to have fun, and they want to be good at something (see chapter 2). Maybe that's why our church mystery meetings are so popular. Whether it's bowling or baseball, kids get involved and bring their friends. Find out what they're interested in and offer to do it with them. In the process, you'll win their respect and love.

"Friendships are also an important part of involvement. Special activities like camping or overnight trips allow a cohesive bond to grow within a group of kids. Loyalties develop, and kids are more likely to become involved in the program itself because they feel comfortable. They feel that they are part of the group. Participation becomes more than going along and being a spectator. Friendship and love draw them into the group, as well as their love and respect for the leader, who encourages them to be part of the group. The program is not as attractive to the kids as is the friendship of the group and their love for their leaders."

From "Youth Ministry Is More Than a Meeting" by E.G. von Trutzschler in *The Youth Leader's Sourcebook*, Gary Dausey, ed. (Grand Rapids: Zondervan Publishing House, 1983).

5. Be Affirming

Everyone wants to be known and to be noticed, especially by people important to them. This goes double for junior highers. Make a point of learning names, greeting kids by name, and offering sincere compliments.

"Hi, Lisa," my wife said as we walked into the sanctuary. "It's good to see you today. We missed you last Sunday. By the way, that's a pretty dress."

"Thank you," Lisa answered. She smiled and joined her parents in the row ahead of us. Lisa and her family have just started attending our church. Gail has tried to make her feel welcome.

Some time ago we had a visitor in Sunday School. At first she didn't want to join us because she didn't know anyone. I assured her that she would fit right in. Then I asked her name. She said she didn't want to tell me because everyone would make fun of it. I said we wouldn't. "Morgan," she whispered. "My name is Morgan."

"That's a great name," I said, and I introduced her to the rest of

"Today we realize that long-term influence with lasting results comes from significant relationships and role models. Of course programming has its place in youth ministry, but the long-term positive influence on the lives of students comes from people, not programs.

"In order to have an important influence in the lives of young people, you do not need to be a dynamic speaker, know all the latest rock musicians, or even dress in the latest fashions. You must, however, love kids and be willing to spend time with them. . . . Caring for your students is the primary prerequisite for working with them."

From *The Youth Builder* by Jim Burns (Eugene, Ore.: Harvest House Publishers, 1988).

the class. They had overheard my assurances to her about her name, so they were polite. During the class, this girl actually volunteered to read a few of the verses aloud. Afterward I thanked her for her reading.

Look for ways to affirm the Lisas and Morgans in your life. You may have heard that Jeff won an award at school, that Dana made the volleyball team, or that Jimmy's project was in the science fair. Go out of your way to congratulate them. It will show that you care. Look through the paper for names and pictures of kids you know. Clip out the picture and mail it with a brief note. They'll love it!

6. Be Aware
Although early adolescents will not talk much about their feelings or about intellectual issues, there will be teachable moments. You never know when they will ask a serious question or want to talk. So you always have to be sensitive and ready to respond at the right time.

- Trudy's grandmother is quite sick.
- Liz didn't make the basketball team.

- Jerome's parents are getting a divorce.
- Bill says he is an athiest.
- Julio asks why there's so much pain and suffering in the world.
- Sharon says she's disgusted by the way kids treat each other at school.
- Robert wonders about evolution.

As you spend time with young people, even the craziest kids will have serious moments or times when they are open to serious thoughts. It would be great if we could predict when those moments will occur. But we can't. So we always have to be ready "to give an answer" (1 Peter 3:15).

HINTS AND WARNINGS

1. *Don't misread body language*

In a long meeting, young people will be restless. It doesn't mean they don't like you or the program; their bodies just have to move. And in a church service, they may look incredibly bored, leaning back, slumped to one side, or leaning forward with head in hand. Of course they may be bored, but that doesn't mean they are against Christianity. And often they just don't know what to do with their arms and legs.

2. *Don't embarrass or make fun of them*

Remember, they are trying to feel good about themselves and they fear looking bad in front of their friends. Give them the chance to succeed in your activities and then praise them for it. Watch out for games that make them look foolish. This is also true for reading and praying aloud. Ask for volunteers or choose those who have volunteered previously.

3. *Contact new kids through friends (whom you know) or at your activities*

Remember, parents and school administrators are very suspicious of adults who hang around kids. When you go to the school, if it's not a public occasion, let the principal know why you're there.

4. Keep track of your contact with individuals

Each time you have a memorable time with someone, jot it down on a file card or a notebook. Keep a record of each young person, listing prayer requests, interests, goals, etc. Also record your observations of the person and your relationship with him or her. This will help ensure against spending all your time with a few people and missing others. At team meetings, you and your fellow youth workers can compare notes and pray for special needs.

> "I would hope to be known as one who loved and built up people—not just programs. It was for people, not programs, that Jesus lived, died, and rose. My legacy must be in lives. Anything less would amount to very little."
>
> Doug Burleigh, President of Young Life International, as quoted in "Campus Life Leader's Guide," May/June 1989.

The key to effective ministry with young people is relationships, getting to know young people personally and letting them know you. With junior highers, this happens by being adult, assertive, available, active, affirming, and aware. Then you will be able to cross this relational bridge with Christ's love.

THINK IT THROUGH

1. If you were starting a junior high ministry from scratch, besides school, where would you meet kids?

2. Considering your (and their) schedule, when would be the best time for you to spend time with kids?

3. Think of the junior high young people you know. What are they interested in? What activities do they enjoy?

4. Considering the interests of your kids, your schedule, and the resources of the community, what activities could you do with small groups of junior highers?

5. As a ministry team, what might be your strategy for building relationships with young people?

CHAPTER 7

GETTING THROUGH

THE MAZE

This chapter is about evangelism, bringing the young person to the Gospel or bringing the Gospel to the young person. As we discussed in chapter 3, it is possible to manipulate children emotionally to get them to make a "decision for Christ." But that would be irresponsible, and I doubt that those decisions would be genuine.

On the other hand, if we believe the Bible, we know the necessity of making a personal commitment to Christ, and we feel the urgency of communicating that message and challenging people to respond. It's a matter of life and death — of heaven or hell.

My point is that we must responsibly and lovingly confront young people with the claims of Christ and call them to commitment to Him. But it won't be easy. In fact, it will seem like the following maze, with barriers at every turn. We may think we're making progress, and then BAM! we hit a wall. In order to know how to respond to these barriers, let's examine each one of them.

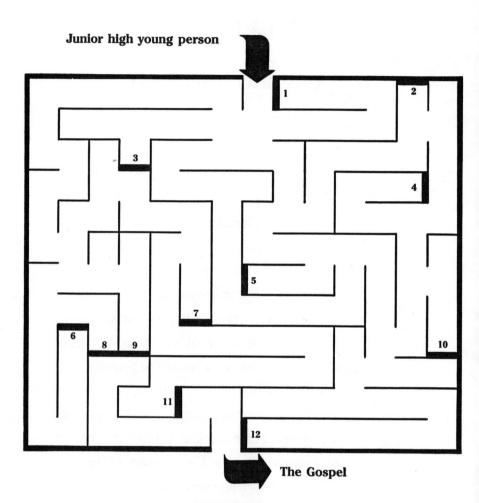

Junior high young person

The Gospel

BARRIERS

1. has short attention span
2. is preoccupied with self
3. is easily distracted
4. has difficult family life
5. doesn't think conceptually
6. is not thinking seriously
7. lacks Bible knowledge
8. is pressured by peers
9. doesn't want to be known as religious
10. has misconceptions about life
11. thinks church is boring
12. has misconceptions about God

COMMUNICATION BARRIERS

1. *Short Attention Span*

Talking to a group of junior highers can be a frustrating, difficult task. Their minds wander and their hands move continually. But consider the young person's plight. It's not easy keeping that growing body still and quiet for very long. Like shaking up an open bottle of Pepsi with your thumb on the top, the energy is just waiting to be released. So don't be surprised if your young people fidget, talk, poke their neighbors, or throw things during a "serious" discussion or your careful explanation of the "Four Spiritual Laws." After all, they have to do *something* with those arms and legs.

The class is going well, I thought as I wrapped up the lesson, telling the Bible story with dramatic flair. For the past few minutes, every junior higher in the class had been quiet and seemed to be listening to everything I had to say. Suddenly Brian's hand shot up, and I thought, *Something I said must have hit home! This will be a good chance to see how much he's understood.*

"Yes, Brian?" I motioned for him to speak.

"What time is it?" he began. "Last week you let us out late . . ."

After regaining my composure—and the class—I made the final point and closed in prayer, wondering if *anything* had gotten through that Sunday.

2. *Preoccupation with Self*

Remember when you were talking with a friend but not really listening because you were thinking of a pressing problem or concern? After an embarrassing pause, you had to answer, "I'm sorry. What did you say?" It's difficult to concentrate when your mind is somewhere else. The same is true of junior highers.

Kids in this age-group are preoccupied with themselves: their looks, performance, feelings, abilities, and so forth. Boys worry about what to wear to school and when their voices will change, and girls spend hours fixing their hair. (Watch a group of junior high girls walk by a mirror or a store window.) And remember, for older students especially, this is when they begin to notice the opposite sex.

You may be talking about commitment, but they may be thinking about cosmetics.

3. *Distractions*

No matter what you're talking about, when something catches the eyes or ears of junior highers, it captures their attention — the toilet flushing upstairs when you meet in the basement, the dog in the back of the family room, the car squealing its tires around the corner, or even a casual reference or illustration in your talk.

In one Sunday School class, I used a movie as an example. Suddenly three or four boys were talking about the movies they had seen recently. In the same class, Andrea interrupted one of my "meaningful monologues" to ask if she could go to the bathroom. In a youth group meeting at someone's home, I forgot to remove the younger sibling's box of stuffed animals from the room. When I turned my back, they became missiles, hurled by boys sitting near the box. Potential distractions are limitless.

4. *Family Tensions*

Let's face it, the American family is in trouble. For years we have heard of rising divorce statistics and the growing number of single-parent families. Add to this the revelations of physical, sexual, and emotional abuse, and we begin to wonder how any child can escape unscarred. Of course it's not all bad — most families, with one or two parents, offer security and nurturing. But don't assume that your group is immune to those problems and tragic situations, especially if you work with a cross-section of kids in the neighborhood.

Even in the *best* families, there are normal stresses and strains, between husband and wife and between parent and child. Frayed nerves, disobedience, accusations, arguments, groundings, and other common household tensions will tend to clutter students' minds and emotions. They will find it difficult to concentrate on your words when they are recovering from a conflict at home.

5. *Concrete, Not Conceptual, Thinking*

Scripture is filled with profound, life-changing concepts. Volumes

"Many young adolescents attend our junior high groups who appear normal and healthy, certainly not abused in any way—yet they may suffer from a lack of support, guidance, and encouragement in the home that will ultimately scar them more severely than physical violence. It's this kind of abuse that's difficult to detect, yet our churches are full of well-meaning parents who, in this way and for whatever reason, abuse their children by default. They are too busy or too tired to spend time with their kids, or they expect someone else to do it for them."

From "Focus on Junior High" by Wayne Rice, *Youthworker*, Fall 1988.

have been written on faith, grace, atonement, justification, redemption, incarnation, sanctification, inspiration, and other deep theological verities. But early adolescents are not thinking conceptually. If the truth is not explained in concrete terms they can understand, they will turn you off quicker than you can say "substitutionary."

6. *Few Serious Thoughts*

This does not mean that junior highers think only about things that are humorous. But seldom do they think about the deeper issues of life, such as meaning, purpose, and the future. One reason for this we have just discussed—junior highers don't think conceptually. But it is also due to their lack of experience and perspective. Up to this point, life has been relatively simple and comfortable for them—their shelter, food, and clothing has been provided by others. And life is exciting as they learn about themselves and the world. Ask a man turning forty to reflect on the meaning of life, and he will have much to say, often through tears. But that question would be nonsense to a child who is just beginning. This is a difficult barrier to overcome, because there's nothing more serious than the Gospel.

7. *Lack of Bible Knowledge*
The gap between the evangelical world and the world at large is growing. Despite the explosion of Christian media, music, and literature, society is becoming increasingly secular. Most children, therefore, have little or no religious background, especially in the Bible. Even kids who have grown up in the church seem to know very little about God's Word. "Gospel," "apostle," "disciple," "Pharisee," "Messiah," "prophet," "cross," and "resurrection" are foreign words to them. So when you read or refer to a Bible passage, chances are your young people won't be able to put it into context or fully appreciate its meaning.

8. *Peer Pressure*
Junior highers are very sensitive to what their friends are thinking and doing. They will cluster and choose a best friend. And the loss of that best friend can be traumatic. Kids can also be cruel with their words, taunting, making fun, and cutting down others. In addition, every group has an unspoken pecking order (even at church). The "leader" sets the pace, and the others follow. Obviously, then, what certain kids think is very important to junior highers. Seldom will they respond individually and openly without regard to what others may think or say.

9. *Aversion to a "Religious" Reputation*
This goes along with the "Peer Pressure" barrier. Many young people begin pulling away from church during the junior high years. And most of their school friends aren't very involved in church. One girl was called "church lady" by a group of boys because she was involved in our youth group. She hadn't been pushy, condescending, or pious. But they mocked her faith. Adults will often do what is right, even if it costs friendships. But young people fear rejection by their peers and will shun anything that might give them a "goody-two-shoes" reputation.

10. *Misconceptions about Life*
As previously mentioned, early adolescents have experienced very little "life" in their 11, 12, or 13 short years. To them pain is

the exception and pleasure is the rule. And *now* is all that counts—five or ten years is an eternity. In addition, they believe that everything revolves around them, their needs and schedules. These and other misconceptions come with being young, but they will be a barrier to any serious discussion of sacrifice, the future, commitment, and selfless service.

11. *Misconceptions about Church*
Many kids see church as boring and irrelevant. The music is slow and dull, the Bible seems old and out of date, and the sermon is long and incomprehensible. They would much rather sit in the back with their friends and pass notes than participate in the service. Instead, they have to sit uncomfortably with the family. Of course, considering their needs and the other barriers described earlier, many of the church programs probably *are* boring and irrelevant. But this idea about church can carry over to any church program. They think, "If the church sponsors it, I won't like it." So they resist going; or, if they do go, they resist listening to what is said.

12. *Misconceptions about God*
Young people also often harbor strange mental pictures of God To many He's an old man, hopelessly out of touch with the 1990s. To some, He's a stern judge, waiting to stop anyone from having fun. To others, God is a great disappointment—they blame Him for physical problems, family situations, or personal tragedies. Those without any church background may form their ideas about God and religion from the caricatures on television and in the movies. And to some, God is simply a concept, impersonal and unknowable. A misconception about God will stand in the way when you are trying to convince a person to give his or her life to Christ.

These are a lot of barriers, and they can be formidable for anyone trying to tell early adolescents about Christ. But effectively communicating the Gospel to junior highers is *not* an unreachable goal. The barriers are not impossible to overcome. Consider the following communication principles.

COMMUNICATION PRINCIPLES

1. *Build a Base*

Professional baseball is a fascinating game to watch if you appreciate the athletic skills needed to play the game and know the strategies involved on the field.

The count is two and two. As the pitcher begins to release the ball, the runner on first breaks to second. Because the batter is left-handed, the shortstop moves to cover second base to take the throw from the catcher. But the batter punches the ball between second and third for a hit, in the space vacated by the shortstop, sending the base runner to third. The play is called a "hit and run," and it's beautiful to watch when executed properly.

Now let's suppose that I am the manager of a Little League team. Having studied the game for years, I decide to teach my young athletes the "hit and run." I would be wasting my time. Instead, I should teach them how to hit and how to run. Only when they've mastered the basics will they be able to move on to more complicated plays.

Or suppose you want to learn a foreign language. In your first class, the teacher gives you a lesson with complicated sentence structure and technical vocabulary. And your assignment is to read a chapter of a book in this new language. That would be ludicrous, because first you must learn the rudimentary aspects of the language, beginning with the alphabet.

Now consider your group of early adolescents. How will you explain incarnation, atonement, and salvation to them? Unless you build a base of knowledge so that they will know what you're talking about, you will be wasting your time. This is especially true for the unchurched. They know nothing about the Bible and very little about Jesus. Another term for this process is "pre-evangelism." Simply stated, it means setting the stage for evangelism, preparing the way for effective communication of the Gospel.

Of course each person and each group is unique. So the first step will be to take a close look at your kids to determine how much they know about God, Jesus, and the Bible. When in doubt, assume that they know very little. Regardless of the group, here are some guidelines to follow:

● Know where you are going with your teaching. In other words, remember that you are laying a foundation for a purpose—to build on it and eventually share the Good News. The basics of the Gospel are: the person of Christ, the reality and consequences of sin, and the necessity for a personal faith-commitment. Decide when and how you will explain these basics. Don't just tell Bible stories that lead nowhere. Have reasons for teaching what you do.

Where Do You Do Evangelism?

"There are two aspects to our evangelistic thrust. During the regular meetings where we talk about life skills, our goal will be pre-evangelism, setting the stage for an evangelistic appeal. We will be giving young people Bible content by using biblical illustrations as we teach life skills. Each of these weekly meetings will have near the end a 'one point message' where we give a simple teaching from Scripture. Again, this is pre-evangelism. This is helping kids who are scripturally illiterate learn more about Jesus and have a basis on which to make a decision. The main evangelistic thrust, however, will be at the big events. The speaker at these events will give a clear Gospel presentation and invite the young people to respond. A three- to four-week small group will be initiated during which the Gospel will be explained clearly and concisely with a question-and-answer time. The young people will be challenged to accept Christ as their personal Savior."

From "Campus Life/JV Newsletter," Dave Veerman, July 1986.

● Use stories from the Bible to illustrate points in your other teaching. For example, if you were telling your group members how to make friends, you could use Jesus' discussion with the woman at the well as an example of how to start a conversation. Although that's not the point of John 4:1-26, telling that story will teach students something about Jesus as they see Him in action. These illustrations will help build their Bible knowledge.

● Center on Christ. Let your young people know that Jesus is both God and man. As a man, He struggled with the same temptations and pressures that they experience. They will be able to identify with a real, historical person.

● Keep your talks short and to the point, keeping in mind the limited attention span of your audience. It is best to have *one* point for each talk. For example, you could tell your class about when Jesus returned to Nazareth and was rejected by his former neighbors and friends. Your point could be that Jesus knew what it was like to be misunderstood and rejected.

● Use literature, video, and other resources to reinforce what you are teaching.

● Make the Bible available. Give away Gospel portions or New Testaments of an easy-to-read version like *The Living Bible*. And then provide a reading plan with the Bible book divided into bite-sized chunks.

Before young people can make a personal commitment to Christ, they have to know who He is. Building a knowledge base means letting them know that Jesus is fully God and fully man; born as a baby in a manger, He came to earth to show us what God is like and to die in our place for all the wrong things we have done; He was tempted just like us but never gave in; He was killed, executed like a criminal by being nailed to a cross; He rose from the dead and is alive today. Of course just knowing those facts doesn't make someone a Christian, but it's a start.

2. *Focus on the Truth*

Although it is tempting to pull emotional strings to get young people to respond, don't do it. Instead, emphasize the *facts* of the Gospel story. Kids must know that they should follow Christ because He is *truth* and His message is *true*, not because they will get something in return.

"There are three major phases in effectively communicating the Gospel to junior high students.

"**Contact** is where we meet kids. This may happen at lunch, at a sporting event, or at a roller skating rink. First impressions are important because junior highers judge immediately. Staff members' love for the Lord and for young people must be real and show through their lives in that first contact.

"**Conduct** is the key. The staff person's life in front of the young person will be one of the first times the Gospel is communicated to him. A junior high school student will take notice of an adult who actually lives differently from the world's standard. As this staff person 'fleshes out' the Gospel, the student will be curious about what makes him or her tick. Overwhelmed by the simple joy, love, and faith of the staff, he will want to find out more.

"**Content** is the handle. The student sees the staff person living the Christian life in front of him, but he will need words to help him understand. The words of the Gospel do exactly that—they give him the verbal handles to the non-verbal actions of the staff."

Greg Johnson, Editor of *Breakaway* (Focus on the Family's junior high magazine).

People play bargaining games with God—"If You get me out of this mess, I'll be good." That's a very immature outlook on God and life, but junior highers are very susceptible to it. They may pray for good grades or to win games, wear a cross for good luck, or "accept Christ" to bring Mom and Dad back together. So don't encourage following Jesus for selfish reasons.

An effective method of communicating with high school and college young people begins with addressing their felt needs. Talking about loneliness, self-concept, fear, sexuality, and so forth will get their attention and open the door to the Gospel. But this approach is usually not very effective with junior highers. They are concentrating on competence, not identity, and their emotions fluctuate greatly. A felt need one moment may be forgotten the next. Lay a factual foundation for commitment to Christ.

When you present the facts of the Gospel, let your young people know that the Christian life isn't all fun and games. In fact, it may involve hardship and difficulties. God does not promise to take us *out* of our problems but *through* them (see John 16:33).

Also let your group members know that they can't depend on anyone else's faith — God has no grandchildren. They are growing up and can make their own decisions. In other words, no matter how little or how much they know about God or have gone to church, each person must make his or her own decision.

Last summer, Kara reported to the church about her experience at camp. As a proud father I heard her say, "I was worried about starting high school this fall, thinking that kids might call me a 'Jesus freak.' But then I thought, 'That's what I am,' and so why should I worry about what they say." Then she asked the congregation to pray for her during the year.

Kara's decision to live for Christ at school was based on her commitment to Christ — the truth — and not on emotion or the prospect of personal gain. It was a significant step in her growth as a Christian.

We follow Christ because the Gospel is *true*, and Christ is the only way (see John 14:6). Give your young people the facts.

3. *Use Words They Understand*
You are a well-educated adult who spends most of your time speaking to other adults about adult concerns. Undoubtedly your vocabulary reflects your maturity and education, as it should. But the vocabulary of most early adolescents is very limited. Remember, some of them only learned to read five or six years ago. Few read books on their own. And even those who are voracious readers often skip over difficult words. (Very few would know what "voracious" means.)

When I decided to dive into the age of information and buy a computer, I had a terrible case of "computer-phobia," intimidated both by the technology and terminology. As I ventured from store to store, the salespersons seemed to be speaking a foreign language—I didn't even know what "hardware" and "software" meant, not to mention RAM, DOS, and bytes. I'm sure that the salespeople wanted to convince me to buy a computer, but they rattled on in computerese, and I was totally confused. Each time I would nod and utter a few "hmmms" as though I understood, and then make my escape as quickly as possible. It wasn't until I read an article in *Consumer Reports* magazine and had a friend explain what everything meant in words I could understand that I overcame my fear and returned to the computer marketplace. If I hadn't been so highly motivated, I would never have bought one.

In the same way, our adult words and Christian clichés can be very intimidating to young people. (And they aren't nearly as motivated as I was.) Remember this when you teach, especially when you come to words like "grace," "mercy," "faith," and "sin." Use different words, or explain what the word means and give relevant examples. Then see if they can define it in their own words or give you another example of what it means. Encourage everyone to ask questions, especially when they don't understand a word, term, or phrase. Effective communication means using language that your listeners understand.

4. *Keep Saying It*
Don't assume that because you've covered a topic once, it has been heard, understood, and applied. You may have to repeat some truths over and over until your young people catch on.

> Individual communication is vital with this age because of the great differences that can exist in one group. There is a vast difference between the typical sixth-grade boy and the typical eighth-grade girl. These differences not only include physical size, but social skills and the ability to think as well.

Some of the barriers described earlier may have kept a person from understanding what you were saying the first three times you said it. But the fourth time, the light goes on, and she responds.

This doesn't mean that you should always tell the Gospel story the same way. Use your imagination and creativity. A young person may respond to a visiting speaker or a personal testimony even though he has heard you give the same message several times. God may use the fresh voice, a different illustration, or a new slant to get through.

Also keep in mind that your junior highers just may not be ready to respond. Salvation is a work of the Holy Spirit, not a response to a clever sales pitch. We must faithfully and responsibly present the message, but God will do the convincing.

During the summer, churches from a number of communities joined together to sponsor a series of evangelistic meetings. The advertised programs featured outstanding music, comedy, testimonies, and a well-known speaker. We took our group on "youth night." The kids stomped, cheered, and clapped to the music, and they laughed hysterically at the comedian's routine. Impressed by the program, I could hardly wait for the speaker, thinking he must be terrific. But I was really disappointed. Although articulate and funny, he seemed to ramble on and on and cover the same territory over and over. And our kids seemed to lose interest, talking, passing notes, and making frequent trips to the bathrooms. You can imagine my shock when, during the invitation, one of our boys went forward—he hadn't seemed to be paying attention at all. But God used something the speaker said to break through, and Todd gave his life to Christ that night.

Present the message clearly and simply, but keep saying it. Be patient. (Being patient also means to keep praying for those who have not yet responded.)

5. Provide Opportunities to Respond
Beyond presenting the message of Christ, you must also provide opportunities for young people to respond, without putting them under great pressure (trying to manipulate them emotionally) or embarrassing them.

"Following my high school Bible study a few weeks ago, I was talking to one of our adult sponsors who had been a missionary overseas. I was telling her that sometimes I feel guilty for not being a missionary to another culture. She shot back, 'You are a missionary to a different culture. These high school kids'—she pointed to a few kids who were still left after the youth group meeting—'live in a different world. You've chosen to infiltrate that world to give them the message of Jesus.' "

From *The Youth Builder* by Jim Burns (Eugene, Ore.: Harvest House Publishers, 1988).

This may be done very naturally on an individual basis. If you have built a relationship with a young person, you can simply ask him what he thought of the talk, or what you have been presenting all year, or about Christ. You could do this after one of the meetings. Or you could explain to the whole group that you want to meet with each one individually, just to see how they're doing. Then no one will feel singled out. (Make this announcement light or humorous so they won't dread the "interview.")

Response cards can also be an effective method for setting up personal appointments. After a meeting, give everyone an index card and ask them to answer a question about the meeting. The question could be as simple as "What are your suggestions for future programs?" or as serious as "From what you learned tonight, what is Jesus like?" Then explain that you or another member of the staff would love to get together with anyone personally to explain more about how to become a Christian, a true follower of Christ. Explain that if people want to get together with you, they should write their names on the bottom of the cards, and then you or someone on your staff will contact them in a day or two. Then collect all the cards. It is important that everyone receives a card and writes something so that no one is singled out. Response cards can also be effective in large group meetings where the speaker can ask for reactions to the message.

Another effective opportunity for response is to invite kids to become involved in a small group where you will discuss how to become a Christian. This group could meet for four weeks, covering one main point of the Gospel at each meeting. The method you use isn't the issue; the important thing is to give kids the chance to respond to Christ's call.

6. *Be Prepared to Share*
You should be ready to take advantage of opportunities that arise as you spend time with kids. Teachable moments often happen when you least expect them, so always be sensitive to the Holy Spirit's leading and ready to respond. This is not to say that you should unload the whole Gospel story each time someone comes to you with a problem, but you should be sensitive to opportunities to share about Christ.

- Marlene sees your Bible in the car and says something about "not being able to understand that book."
- George declares that he doesn't believe in all that "God stuff" because he's never seen God.
- Toni wonders about some preacher she heard about on the news.
- Estelle says she went to church once with her grandmother, a long time ago, but hasn't been back since.
- Brent asks a question about prayer.
- Philip is visibly upset over his parents' impending divorce.

God will give you opportunities to share the Good News. Be ready.

7. *Be Prepared to Lead*
You should also be prepared to lead a young person to Christ. Evangelism is not just presenting the "whats," "whys," and "hows" of the Gospel—it is also personally introducing young people to Christ. Be sure to think through the process, what you will tell the person to do and how you will pray.

Here's a quick summary of what I do. After explaining the process, I usually pray first, aloud, thanking God for this special young person and asking Him to give the person the courage and faith to make this commitment. Next I have the person pray aloud, expressing sorrow for sin and gratitude for what Jesus did on the cross and then asking God to come in and take over his or her life. Then I pray again, thanking God for what He has just done in this person's life. Afterward, I ask the person to explain what just happened, and I encourage him or her to tell a Christian friend about his or her new relationship with Christ.

Be ready to share the Good News and to lead kids to Christ.

8. *Be Prepared to Follow Through*

Remember, accepting Christ as Saviour is just the first step in the Christian walk. Therefore, it is important to plug new believers into a program that will help them grow in the faith. This may mean getting them involved in a small group, giving them a workbook to finish, meeting with them regularly, or a combination of the above. The point is, have a plan.

Follow-through also means communicating with parents and helping kids adjust at home. If the young person comes from a Christian home, Mom and Dad will probably be very supportive of their son or daughter's decision. Work with them and make discipleship a team effort.

If, however, the young person comes from a non-Christian home, you will need to help him or her translate the experience into words his or her parents would understand. Encourage the person to *live* for Christ at home instead of walking in the door and making an announcement.

Follow-through should also involve the church. Give young people opportunities to participate in the larger body of believers. If they don't go to your church, encourage them to get involved in one, while respecting the wishes of their parents.

Be prepared to share the message, to lead young people to Christ, and to follow through.

THE KEY

If you tried to follow the maze at the beginning of this chapter, you found that there was no way through. Every route on the paper was blocked. That wasn't a mistake. I designed the maze that way to illustrate the fact that on our own we can't break through and bring a young person to Christ. In fact, the solution to the maze is to go *over* it, not *through*—and that means PRAYER.

Enlist the prayer support of fellow believers. And pray as a ministry team:
- for individuals;
- for programs and activities;
- for opportunities to share;
- for wisdom to overcome communication barriers;
- for sensitivity to individuals and opportunities;
- for spiritual power;
- for faithfulness to God's Word and to responsible evangelism.

"You'd better have a deep love for these young people. If you don't, they will see through you so fast! Do junior high ministry because you love junior high students. If junior high ministry is your step to 'bigger and better' things, please do yourself, your church, and the precious junior high students a big favor and get out."

Scott Pederson, Director of Sonlight Express, Willow Creek Community Church (South Barrington, Illinois).

Satan will do all he can to hinder communication of the Gospel. And he has weapons at his disposal in addition to the barriers outlined at the beginning of the chapter. But Satan is no match for God. Bathe your ministry in prayer.

Whether you minister in the neighborhood or in church, you will meet junior high kids who do not know Christ. They need to give their lives to Him—it's a matter of life and death. Of course these young people must be handled with care, but they are not too young to follow Christ. Make responsible evangelism a part of your ministry plan.

THINK IT THROUGH

1. What barriers tend to keep the junior highers you know from listening to the Gospel or to a lesson from God's Word?

2. Think of the junior high kids in your life. What do they need to know about themselves, God, and Jesus to give them a good base for making a personal commitment to Christ?

3. Translate the phrase "accept Christ as your personal Saviour' into words that junior highers could understand.

4. Besides speaking to them, what other methods could you use to communicate the Gospel to a group of early adolescents?

5. Suppose a young person asked you to lead him or her to Christ. What would you do?

6. What resources do you have for following through with new believers?

CHAPTER 8

GETTING TOGETHER

They just kept coming — Mary and two friends, Carol, Tommy and his neighbor, Linda, Justine, Craig, James — each one greeted warmly by members of the ministry team. Soon, fifty (normal attendance was in the twenties) eager and enthusiastic young people packed the room, laughing and talking among themselves. Jeff stepped to the front, and as though on cue, the crowd quieted to hear his opening comments.

Jeff welcomed everyone, described the first game, and divided the group into teams. Kids quickly organized and then cheered as teammates passed shaving cream from nose to nose. The next crowdbreaker was a spirited bubble gum race, seeing who could be the first to blow and pop a three-inch bubble. Then the group searched for unique items in an indoor scavenger hunt.

After quieting everyone, Jeff introduced the slide presentation, a study in loneliness. The lights dimmed, and the projector flashed a series of somber images with a blues song serving as background. Then, turning on the lights again, Jeff asked for the group's reactions and led a lively discussion on life's lonely moments.

With the discussion setting the stage, Jeff wrapped up by explaining how Christ could be their friend and bring them through their lonely times. Then he distributed index cards so that they could register their reactions and indicate whether they wanted to have a personal appointment with a staff member.

After collecting the cards and pencils, Jeff thanked the group for coming and sent them to refreshments. Quickly flipping through the react cards, he saw that six kids had indicated their desire to know more about Christ.

"What a meeting!" thought Jeff . . . then he woke up.

Most youth leaders dream of such a meeting, where attendance is great, the projector works, kids are attentive, everything goes right, and everyone responds positively. But usually that's just a dream. In fact, many meetings resemble nightmares instead — much like this:

Jeff was expecting twenty, but ten kids (and no one else from the ministry team) straggled in and sat at the edges of the room, talking loudly among themselves. Carol was reading and laughing over notes that Todd had written to Justine, and Tommy was picking dirt out of the bottoms of his Nikes (the dirt pile was almost as high as a shoe). After three unsuccessful tries, Jeff finally got the group's attention and divided them into two teams over loud objections. The first game quickly deteriorated into a mini shaving cream fight, until the cans were confiscated. As for the bubble gum race, no one was able to blow a bubble, so it was declared a draw. The scavenger hunt began well, but soon became chaotic when everyone began charging to the front with each item.

Jeff decided to move to the slides, but soon discovered that no one was watching. Mercifully, the bulb burned out. The discussion and wrap-up followed suit, with Jeff spending most of his energy trying to get everyone quiet. And when he distributed index cards, handmade airplanes filled the air as he searched for the pencils. Finally, in disgust, Jeff dismissed the meeting, and watched everyone stampede to the refreshment table.

Meetings and special events can be valuable ministry tools, providing a place for finding fun, friends, food, and faith. But good meetings don't happen automatically. They take good planning and then proper execution.

MEETING PLANS

The Objective

As we discussed in chapter 3, the first step in creating effective meetings is planning; and a good plan begins with an objective. In other words, you should think through the purpose of the meeting, what you want it to accomplish, and then write out your objective.

Obviously, effective meetings can help you achieve the goals of your youth ministry. Specifically, they can help accomplish this in four different ways.

1. They can build a sense of identity and unity, giving kids a place to belong.

2. They can provide an accepting atmosphere, allowing kids to speak their minds and to be themselves.

3. They can offer good, clean fun.

4. They can communicate biblical content.

The first three are accomplished in the *way* the event is run, including the setting and atmosphere. Numbers 1 and 2 will govern how you welcome kids and make them feel at home. And they will determine the ground rules for how you expect kids to treat each other. Number 3 will affect your choice of activities and how you run them. In essence, those three goals are usually beneath the surface, unspoken. But they should be considered when planning any event.

Number 4, however, is the most important one to consider when writing your objective statement. What do you want kids to know or do as a result of the event? If your goal is evangelism, you could write: "As a result of this meeting, kids will know what it means to become a Christian, and will be given the opportunity to respond." If your meeting is about family relationships, your objective could read: "As a result of this meeting, kids will express love for their parents by writing thank-you letters to them."

If you have a clear and concise objective, the meeting will be easy to plan as you evaluate each part of the meeting in light of that objective.

The Timing
Next, you should think through the timing of the event—*backward.* First decide when you want the meeting to end and make sure you have time for the most important parts. The whole meeting should be designed to meet your objective, but certain ingredients are more important than others for effective communication. Many times I've been in large rallies where a well-known speaker was flown in at great expense. As a trained and experienced professional, he was hired to bring a Gospel challenge. But the program was so cluttered with music, skits, announcements, and games that by the time the speaker was introduced, everyone was ready to go home. Too often we get so carried away with our games and creativity that there is no time for the heart of the meeting.

It is also important to use program ingredients that enhance, not detract, from the message. Don't expect kids to go bananas one second and listen quietly the next. Think about how you can set up the speaker or teacher and make communication more effective. Whatever you use to communicate the content, make sure that the rest of the meeting flows toward it. Good timing is critical.

The Response
It's also important to think through how you want kids to respond, what you want them to do. Will you give them an assignment to carry out during the week? Do you want them to talk with staff? Will you ask them to fill out a react card? Will you have them pray? Of course, how you want the group to respond will be directly related to your meeting objective.

MEETING PRINCIPLES
As you design your meeting, be sure to keep these principles in mind. They apply to any junior high event.

Fun with a Purpose

"Kids say the #1 reason they come to youth group is to have fun. But youth leaders say their #1 priority is to encourage Christian growth. Are the two mutually exclusive? I don't think so. Church-centered entertainment has real ministry value. Here's why:

1. Youth group activities are a positive alternative to an often negative social environment. Young people have a critical need to develop strong, healthy social relationships. And entertaining social events can be just as important as spiritual and academic training.

2. Entertaining activities help kids learn how to play. Fierce competition and structured athletics have hurt kids' ability to create their own fun. Good social programming can teach teenagers the power of positive partying. They can learn how to have a good time without drugs, sex, or alcohol."

From "Are You an Entertainer or a Minister?" by Scott Noon, *Group Magazine,* April/May 1989.

1. *Make the meeting active*

Because junior highers are so filled with energy, they will not sit still for long periods of time. But instead of fighting their energy, take advantage of it by employing active games that you can control, and by not having them sit very long for any part of the meeting.

Early adolescents' energy can be a blessing or a curse. They can have fun with almost anything you do. In fact, two junior high boys will chase themselves all over the lawn at any given moment. So you don't have to plan complicated and sophisticated activities to entertain them. But their energy can also destroy a meeting if you're not careful. Let them get some of the energy out of their systems, but don't let them get out of control.

2. *Move the meeting along*
Because these young people have such short attention spans, divide your meeting into 5–7 minute segments. This can be done even in a Bible study. You could begin by using games that are discussion starters and then break into small groups for answering questions from Scripture. This could be followed with a quiz over the information just learned in a game show format. Then kids could apply the lesson by analyzing case studies. You could conclude the meeting with a challenge and prayer. Also, each program should have a tight structure with no gaps between elements. Move from one part into the next, quickly and smoothly.

3. *Keep everything simple*
This principle applies to the whole event and to each part. The procedures and rules of your games should be easy to explain, and the meeting should move in a straight line toward achieving the objective. Explain the meeting to a friend. If he seems confused, so will your junior highers, so simplify it.

4. *Taper the meeting*
This relates to the timing of the meeting as described earlier. Schedule your more active and loud games first; then follow with ones that are a little less involved. This will help with crowd control and will allow you to get your group's attention for serious communication.

In the meeting described at the opening of this chapter, Jeff preceded his slide show with an indoor scavenger hunt. What a mistake! After running around the room and cheering loudly, it's almost impossible for junior highers to suddenly get quiet and serious, especially with the lights off.

5. *Allow time for socializing*
Junior highers are just discovering what it means to be social, and they want to talk to each other. Provide time for this, before the meeting and afterward. One church's youth group meetings are scheduled to begin at 6:30 and end at 8:00. The meetings themselves last only about 45 minutes, beginning at 6:45 and

Building Excitement in Programs

Excitement is based on the following factors:
1. a past history of excitement (it'll snowball)
2. music playing as your young people enter the room
3. what you say as you open the meeting
4. the type of crowdbreaker that you begin with (a big opener!)
5. how you explain the instructions
6. the time limits
7. giving everyone the chance to move around
8. music playing as the crowdbreaker is happening
9. the progression of the crowdbreakers
10. group members seeing themselves in slides or videos
11. how much group members' friends are part of the meeting
12. your attitude ("I'm gonna have fun!")
13. how well you publicize and psyche your kids up for future activities
14. how you relate to the other staff during the meeting
15. how well you're heard
16. doing the unexpected
17. playing on school spirit
18. lighting, room temperature, decorations (posters and banners).

ending at 7:30. Afterward, there are refreshments. Kids can social-ize during the fifteen minutes before, as everyone arrives, and the half hour after, during refreshments.

Social events will also help meet this need. That's one of the reasons we have mystery meetings for our church youth group. They offer opportunities for fun and for being with friends.

6. *Think through every aspect*
The idea here is to anticipate potential problems so that you can

prevent them. Ask yourself what could possibly go wrong with each meeting element, and think how your kids will probably

---

Tips for Junior High Meetings

1. Don't use paper. Some kids will crumple it or make it into paper planes immediately. Instead, use index cards or larger pieces of card stock.

2. Pick up all props immediately after using them. Kids will find ingenious alternate uses for them.

3. Make sure all the games are fair. Every kid thinks he or she is a lawyer and will accuse you and the other team of cheating if he or she is losing.

4. Watch out for lopsided scores. This will deflate any contest. You could stop the game early and declare the winner; then start a new game, giving the losing team another opportunity. (You may want to reorganize the teams at this time.) Or you could use creative scoring, awarding double points later in the game.

5. Keep soft drinks cold and then serve them in cups, without ice. Cubes usually find their way down others' backs, and cans get sprayed around the room.

6. Get to the meeting place early to arrange the room the way you want it.

---

respond. This analysis should also include the setting, staff, equipment, and props. Is there enough room for everyone? What kind of distractions could there be? What will you do with the broken balloon pieces? Where will you store the props until you need them? How will you set up the projector and screen without having them be in the way during the rest of the meeting? Who will get the refreshments ready and when will they do it? How can you be sure the room temperature is comfortable?

A few years ago we held our Campus Life/JV "Float Soak" (the kick-off event featuring free root beer floats) in the lower gym at the school. The room was used for wrestling and broom hockey and had a cement floor. Besides being uncomfortable, the room was very noisy. In addition, some of the boys brought their skateboards. You can imagine the crowd control problems we had. I could have saved myself a lot of grief if I had checked out the room ahead of time and had foreseen the potential problems.

Taking time to think through and think ahead will help you run a smooth and effective program.

MEETING PARTS
We've discussed meeting plans and meeting principles, now let's take a look at some specific meeting ingredients.

Crowdbreakers
As the name implies, the main purpose of crowdbreakers is to "break the crowd." In other words, these games should break down social barriers, help kids get to know each other, and build the group. Crowdbreakers can include competitive games, group tasks, songs—just about anything that involves everyone and is fun. These activities don't have to be tied to the theme of the meeting, but they should help you achieve your objective. For example, their main purpose may just be to establish the right atmosphere for communication.

When choosing or creating crowdbreakers, ask yourself the following questions:

● **Will this be fun?** Your group may participate because you ask them, but ideally you want them to enjoy what they're doing. Kids should look forward to this time of the meeting. Picture yourself in their place and ask: "If I were in junior high and with this group, would I enjoy doing this?"

● **Will this be fun for everyone?** Don't use crowdbreakers that favor the bigger and stronger kids, making the smaller

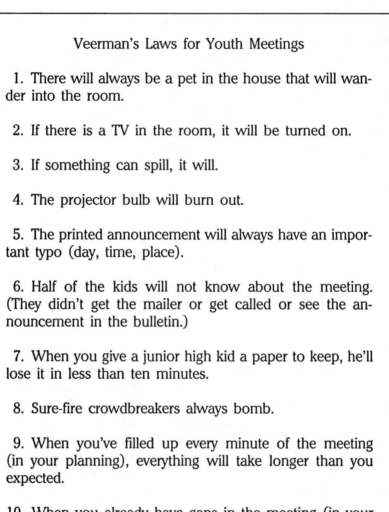

Veerman's Laws for Youth Meetings

1. There will always be a pet in the house that will wander into the room.

2. If there is a TV in the room, it will be turned on.

3. If something can spill, it will.

4. The projector bulb will burn out.

5. The printed announcement will always have an important typo (day, time, place).

6. Half of the kids will not know about the meeting. (They didn't get the mailer or get called or see the announcement in the bulletin.)

7. When you give a junior high kid a paper to keep, he'll lose it in less than ten minutes.

8. Sure-fire crowdbreakers always bomb.

9. When you've filled up every minute of the meeting (in your planning), everything will take longer than you expected.

10. When you already have gaps in the meeting (in your planning), everything will go more quickly than you expected.

ones losers or leaving them on the sidelines. Choose non-discriminatory activities. Games with blindfolds and unusual rules can put everyone on the same level. And in group tasks, everyone works together to accomplish a goal.

Don't choose activities that only a few kids appreciate. Sometimes quizzes fall into this category. A few kids may enjoy them while everyone else is bored. Of course, everyone doesn't have to actively participate to be involved. You can have contests with two or three competitors at the front of the room while the rest of the crowd watches, laughs, and cheers.

● **Will this affirm kids?** Beware of anything that may embarrass individuals. With growing and often awkward bodies, fragile egos, and glaring social needs, junior highers need to be built up, not torn down. Use crowdbreakers to give them opportunities to succeed, not to fail. This doesn't mean that everyone will win every game—in any competition, someone has to lose. But instead of treating them as "losers," treat them as "runners-up" and compliment them on trying and on doing well, even though they didn't "win."

This whole area of competition should be handled with care. Competition can be healthy and can motivate the group to participate and succeed—if the competition is kept in check. If you use teams, *don't* let the kids choose or divide up on their own. Instead, consider the easiest way to divide the kids so that the teams are evenly matched. You could have one half of the room against the other, boys against girls, sixth and seventh graders against eighth graders (if the numbers are equal), and so forth. Or you could just place kids where you want them. If these teams will be competing in a series of events, award points for every place so that no team is blown out. Last Sunday, for example, we began youth group with a series of competitions between two teams. In each game, the winning team received 2,000 points and the other team 1,000.

Also, don't make winning a big deal by making a grand announcement and awarding a super prize. We usually just acknowledge the winning team or let them get in line first for refreshments. These kids want to win, but they really aren't that concerned about being "grand champions of all time." In fact, at one of our Campus Life/JV area events, we formed new teams for every contest: by schools, birthdays, ages, color of clothing, etc. Everyone still competed hard in every game.

• **Will this be easy to explain, run, and control?** As mentioned earlier, everything in the meeting should be as simple as possible. Lengthy and complicated explanations will lose most of the kids; numerous props will be broken, lost, or used as missiles; and chaotic or wild games will destroy the meeting.

At one event, I had a game where each person was supposed to have five balloons tied to his or her arms and legs. You can imagine what happened as I distributed strings and balloons to the crowd of 75. No one understood what to do, and they began popping each other's balloons as soon as they were inflated. Then they began chasing each other around the room. I had to quickly confiscate all the props and move on to another game.

One of the great things about junior highers is that they are easy to entertain. You don't have to have complicated and creative crowdbreakers to get them involved. At a recent youth group, the guys asked if they could play tag in the field before we began. And they are always asking to repeat popular crowdbreakers from other meetings. Keep everything simple.

• **Will this facilitate communication?** In other words, will this crowdbreaker move the group *toward* or *away* from the goals you want to accomplish? Everyone may love a shaving cream fight, but I doubt that it would help you study the Bible together. Keep the meeting objective in mind as you choose the crowdbreakers.

• **Will this model the right values?** Nothing in your meetings should contradict the values and priorities you are teaching. Don't do anything which could go in a different direction. Often team leaders are more competitive than the kids. This is especially true for younger leaders who often will do almost anything to help their teams win. I have seen youth directors argue with referees in basketball games and cheat at volleyball. What messages do those actions communicate? On the other hand, think about how leaders could turn losing into winning by encouraging and affirming team members, playing fair, and having a good attitude. Make sure that the staff understands whose needs are being met.

For the content of your meetings . . .

1. Focus on early adolescent relationships rather than issues. If you deal with the issues that arise out of their relationships (friends, authority figures, parents, etc.), you will find young people more readily able to put the concepts into practice in their own lives.

2. When planning the content of your meetings, do not assume that these young people know a lot of facts and related material, including Bible content. Do not assume that they understand basic truths or basic principles. They may be able to repeat the principles but have no idea what they really mean.

3. Gear your content to the maturity levels which are evident in your group. Junior highers can range in maturity from very, very childish to quite adult acting and sophisticated.

Sandy Jones, Junior High Club Director, Central Florida Youth for Christ.

Also, stay away from all sexual innuendos and bathroom humor. Junior high boys are notorious for talking gross, so you can get easy laughs with certain jokes or comments. But that's the wrong direction. Don't do it and don't allow it. How you run the games, how you treat kids, and how you talk and act will say much about you and your values.

● **What are the strengths of the meeting place and how can I use them?** Take advantage of your environment; don't fight it. If the weather is good, go outside for the first part of the meeting. Every setting can be used for crowdbreakers. A park may have playground equipment, pinecones, insects, trees, and athletic fields. A church may have a piano, chalkboards, folding chairs, hymnals, and Sunday School supplies. A family room may have children's toys, a Ping-Pong table, VCR, easy access to a kitchen, and old clothes. Take advantage of what you have.

Although you will use more games in some meetings than in others, try to have at least one crowdbreaker in every meeting, even in Sunday School. In Sunday School you could open with a contest that would help you review what you have covered (e.g., "Wheel of Fortune," "Hangman," scrambled words from memory verses, etc.) or introduce the topic of the day (e.g., collages, lists, songs, etc.). And you could end your class with another game *if* you have time (this can serve as an incentive for your young people to help you get through the lesson). For one quarter, we ended each Sunday School class with a Bible drill, boys against the girls. The kids loved it! I thought it was old, but they had never done it before.

Other Discussion Starters

In addition to crowdbreakers and games, other group activities can help prepare the group for discussion, Bible study, or a wrap-up. These include simulation games, role plays, group reactions, instant dramas, and pictures. Videos can be very effective, especially if you stop the tape in the middle of the story and discuss with your group what has happened and what they think will happen next. However, be sure to preview all videos before you show them.

Young people seem to be obsessed with music. Use this to your advantage in the meetings. Play a popular song and ask what a certain phrase means. Or talk about the kinds of values the singers portray through their lifestyles.

I have found that junior highers love to be in the spotlight, on stage. Again, capitalize on this interest. Beforehand, choose kids to act out a special mini-drama or role play in front of the whole group. This can be an effective way to focus on typical situations at school or at home, to bring Bible stories to life, or to solve typical interpersonal problems. Be sure to choose the right kids for these plays, and give them opportunity to rehearse or to think about

The Difference the Differences Make

"The differences between junior and senior high students create a chasm. The latter see sixth through eighth graders as emotionally immature, socially uncool, intellectually shallow, and generally not with it. Junior highers often feel socially snubbed, intellectually outwitted, and physically outdone by the older kids. A separate, unique program is necessary to reach junior high students.

"Careful attention should be made to keep the junior high program distinctly different from the high school program. To some extent this will occur naturally as we attempt to meet their needs, but it is important that activities and games which are traditionally used in the high school ministry are not used here. After two or three years in a junior high program, students should move on to something new and fresh in high school."

Greg Johnson, Editor of *Breakaway* (Focus on the Family's junior high magazine).

what they will say. Otherwise you may have someone just stand at the front and giggle.

Discussions
Whether or not it is possible to have effective discussions with junior highers depends a lot on the ages of the kids in the group and their intellectual development. Some will enjoy talking about biblical themes, felt needs, and life. But many will become quickly bored with discussions of any depth.

Discussions can help kids get involved in meetings and think through issues, if they are handled right. Here are some guidelines for effective discussions.

1. Keep the issues concrete, focused, and life-related. If

A Moving Target

"This is a time of rapid change—young people are not only changing in themselves from week to week, but no two junior highers will experience this changing in the same way. Programs aimed at the needs of a particular age group may or may not hit a junior higher, simply because he's a moving target. We need to make sure our programs and activities vary sufficiently to give junior highers the individual attention they need."

From "Focus on Junior High" by Wayne Rice, *Youthworker Journal*, Spring 1988.

---

you ask what "grace" means to them, you will be met with silence. But if you ask for examples of how teachers are unfair at school, you will get an earful.

One very effective discussion starter is to use case studies of other junior high kids. You could say something like: "At church, Kenny learned that as a Christian, he should be loving and kind to others. The next day, Monday, he was walking down the hall at school when he saw Barry being picked on by some older boys. They were knocking his books out of his hands and making fun of him. What should Kenny do?" After they respond, ask: "What would you do?"

Or you could say: "Mary is having a tough time in math. Her teacher, Mr. Reed, seems to always pick on her. He won't let her do extra credit to improve her grade, and once he even accused her of cheating when she wasn't. What should Mary do?" Then ask: "What would you do?"

Kids will discuss issues related to their lives and situations in which they can identify with the kids in the story.

2. Ask short questions that have short answers. Such questions can help you focus on a specific Bible passage. Looking at

Luke 4:16-30, you could ask: "How did the people in Jesus' home-town treat Him?" "Why?" "How did Jesus respond to what they did?"

What you don't want to do is ask a question like: "What happened when Jesus returned to His hometown?" That's a little too long and open-ended.

I must quickly add, however, that you should avoid "yes/no" questions. Those are short answers, but they require very little thinking. Recently I overheard a Sunday School teacher leading a discussion by asking questions like: "When the disciples saw what happened, they didn't like it, did they?" (Answer: no.) "Do you think Jesus knew that would happen?" (Answer: yes.) "That's right. And He knows what will happen in our lives too, doesn't He?" (Answer: yes.) "Have you ever felt like the disciples?" (Answer: silence and then a few mumbled yeses.)

If a question is worth asking, usually it can be stated in a way that would avoid a simple yes/no answer. For example, the last question the well-meaning Sunday School teacher asked could have been rephrased: "When have you felt like the disciples, angry and confused?"

And here's another tip if you are in a church setting. Don't ask questions that can be answered with the usual Sunday School answers, "Jesus," "God," or "the Bible." From their earliest years, children who grow up in church learn that those answers are usually right for almost every question they're asked.

3. Ask questions that move you in the right direction. Instead of one large question, think of a series of smaller ones that head the right way. Let's say that your topic is how to improve relationships with parents. Instead of asking, "What can you do to improve relationships at home?" you could ask:

"What kinds of things do you and your parents usually fight about?"

"How do those arguments usually end?"

"Who wins?"

"Let's take that one area of cleaning your room. What might you do to stop an argument about that before it happens?"

4. Divide into groups of 5–7 people. The goal of a good discussion is to get everyone involved. In a large group, this is impossible—either everyone will be talking at once, or most of the group will lose interest while a few discuss the issue. By breaking into smaller groups, each with an adult leader, you will be able to get participation from almost everyone. Of course, this will mean that you will have to prepare ahead of time with your staff, giving them the questions to ask in the groups. If you reassemble as a large group for reports, have the adult leaders give quick, concise summaries of what each group discussed and decided.

Dividing into groups will also help you with crowd control. One junior high Sunday School class I know of is organized around four tables. Each table has five kids and a leader. In another church with a very large junior high department, the group is broken down into many classes.

5. Establish clear ground rules. Let everyone know what is acceptable and unacceptable behavior during your discussions. Here are some examples.
- Only one person may speak at a time.
- You may speak only when the leader recognizes you after you have raised your hand.
- No gross talk or swearing is allowed.
- No cutting down others is allowed.
- Be quiet and listen when someone else is talking.

Come to an agreement on your rules and write them out as a contract. Let your students give their input on the rules.

Also, during the discussion, you should act as moderator and facilitator, and not give your opinions or the answers or take sides. Never condemn or comment negatively on an answer—you'll lose the student. This doesn't mean you shouldn't challenge a wild or weird statement or bring the discussion back on track. But try to be neutral and to accept each young person's answer. After the meeting you can tell them what you think or show them what the Bible says. Use discussions to get kids thinking about important issues and to set the stage for communication.

What Our Lives Preach

"Our activities mean more than just good, clean fun. They provide action models of the Christian life. In an activity with students, our actions will speak very loudly. Here we can demonstrate mature Christian values and attitudes. If we cheat while playing a game of football with the students and then during the meeting tell them about the importance of being honest, they will be more likely to remember and follow our actions, not our words. On the other hand, if we play fairly and do not lose our cool when we drop a pass or blow a play, the students will see our attitudes and want to imitate them. Remember, we are models. Many of the students are patterning their lives after us. When honesty is discussed in the meeting, the students will have a better understanding of its importance because they have just seen it demonstrated in football."

Greg Johnson, Editor of *Breakaway* (Focus on the Family's junior high magazine).

Bible Studies

Some of your meetings will center on the Bible. It is important that your young people know God's Word, what it teaches, and how to study it. (We will discuss this in more depth in chapter 10.) Here are some guidelines for incorporating Bible study into your meetings.

- Use an understandable translation of the Bible and make sure everyone has a copy.
- Help them find their way around the Bible (most don't know the books of the Bible).
- Don't embarrass poor readers by surprising them and having them read aloud. Give your readers time to practice before the meeting.
- Study one story or paragraph at a time. In other words, keep

the lessons short and simple—don't try to cover the whole Old Testament in one quarter.
• Put the passage in its historical and cultural setting. As I've mentioned before, most kids, even church kids, know very little about the Bible or have any sense of history.
• Find the biblical principles—the timeless truths—in each passage and show how those principles apply to the lives of young people today.
• Help students design action plans to put the lessons into practice.

Wrap-Ups
Talking to junior highers can be intimidating. But there comes a time when someone has to summarize, teach, and challenge—in other words, speak to them. How can you keep the attention of a restless group of adolescents who are probably uncomfortable and thinking of refreshments? And then how can you connect, communicating God's life-changing message?

It's not easy. Don't assume that because they like you or be-

---

Some Social Differences Between Junior High and Senior High Students

1. The junior high student is more interested in antisocial acts just to see what will happen. Generally, the high school student knows and has deliberately chosen to do a certain act.
2. The junior high student is extremely critical and often unkind in his remarks. The high school student has more manners and a higher regard for the feelings of others.
3. Junior high students tend to form their own cliques more than high school students.
4. Junior high students are still trying to find themselves, while high school students are farther down the road physically and emotionally.

cause you're the leader, they will pay attention. Often they can't help themselves from moving around or talking with friends. But you *can* get through.

Of course your task will be much easier if the rest of the meeting has been designed properly, because the students will be prepared to hear what you have to say. But even if everything has gone perfectly, and your young people are quiet and ready to listen, you have to be careful or you will lose them. As you prepare and deliver your talk, remember these suggestions.

1. Make one point (two at the most). Don't unload the whole counsel of God in one talk. Decide on the most important truth you want to communicate and then concentrate on that. Cover the next step or additional truths in future meetings.

2. Use object lessons or case studies. The more concrete examples you can use, the better. When talking about peer pressure, I will often bring a balloon and show how it reacts to being squeezed from one side and then the other. It gives in and bulges out the other side. ("Sometimes we feel like that, don't we?") Eventually it pops under pressure from all sides. Then I bring out a basketball and try the same kinds of external pressures. The point is that we need strength on the inside to withstand the pressures from the outside.

All around us there are objects that we can use: a nail (crucifixion of Christ), a cocoon (new life), a leaf or flower (the wonders of creation), a flashlight (direction, guidance), books, dirt, pictures, bicycle spokes, computer software, string, eraser, etc. Use your imagination.

Case studies and true-life examples will also be effective. Look for news stories about young people. Or write your own case studies. Young people also enjoy stories. Whether it's a fable or the story of a junior high student in another town, they will listen if you tell it well. Your own testimony fits into this category.

3. Keep it short. Don't ramble on, making the same point over and over in one talk. Think in terms of speaking for 5–7 minutes.

Only if you are an experienced speaker who knows how to keep junior highers' attention through humor, illustrations, and stories should you go longer. Your talk should wrap up what has already happened in the meeting, as opposed to being sermon-length and introducing three new points.

4. Use a personal tone. Avoid preaching at these kids. Instead, talk with them. Don't demand their attention because you are in charge; gain their attention because of who you are—someone who cares about them—and because of what you have to say.

5. Have them respond. Whether you are presenting a Bible lesson or an evangelistic challenge, it is important to give kids a chance to respond, to put into action what they have learned. Use react cards, questionnaires, assignments, raised hands, appointment cards, or some other method to reinforce your teaching.

Because junior highers love to get together and to have fun, meetings and other events can be key elements in the ministry. To have "dream" meetings instead of nightmares, plan carefully—assembling the parts and remembering the principles—to meet your objectives.

THINK IT THROUGH

1. What would you like to see your youth group meetings accomplish?

2. Where will you hold these meetings? How often will you meet?

3. What advantages and disadvantages does that meeting place have?

4. How will you divide the responsibilities in a typical meeting among the ministry team?

5. What resources do you have for crowdbreakers, discussion starters, discussions, Bible studies, skits, plays, videos, music, and wrap-ups?

6. If you or your church has very few of those resources, where can you get them?

7. What role will kids play in planning and running the meetings?

CHAPTER 9

THE HOW-TOS

MODEL (mäd-l) n. [L *modus*, a measure] 1. a small representation of a planned or existing object 2. a person or thing regarded as a standard of excellence to be imitated 3. a style or design 4. one who poses for an artist or photographer or who is employed to display clothes by wearing them v. 1. to serve as a model 2. to represent others of the same style

ROLE MODEL (fōl mäd-l) n. a person so effective or inspiring in some social role, job, etc. as to be a model for others

VALUE (val-yü) n. [L *valere*, be worth] 1. the worth of a thing in money or goods 2. estimated worth 3. purchasing power 4. that quality of a thing which makes it more or less desirable, useful, etc. 5. a thing or quality having intrinsic worth 6. [pl.] beliefs or standards 7. relative duration, intensity, etc.

TEACH (tēch) v. 1. to show how to do something; give lessons to 2. to give lessons in (a subject) 3. to provide with knowledge, insight, etc.

SKILL (skil) n. 1. great ability or proficiency 2. a: an art, craft, etc., especially one involving the use of the hands or body b: ability in such an art, etc.

(Adapted from *Webster's New World Dictionary*, New York: Warner Books, 1984.)

In chapter 3 I said that in ministering to junior highers we should model values and teach skills. Now that we've defined our terms, let's look a little closer at what it all means.

MODEL VALUES

Simply stated, a value is something of worth. Our values, therefore, are those things, qualities, or beliefs that are valuable to us—possessions, people, activities, ideas, truths.

And "modeling" means representing or living out—providing a living demonstration. So "modeling values" means living out what is important to us.

Regardless of what we say, we communicate our values by how we act and react. Compare your reactions to a broken lightbulb and a dented automobile. Undoubtedly you would be much more upset over the car than the bulb because it's worth more. You value the automobile more highly.

We also demonstrate what is valuable to us by how we treat things. My computer is valuable to me, so I keep it secure, clean, and covered. But I don't care that much about my old running shoes, so they lie in a corner of the garage.

In addition, we speak volumes by how we spend our time, especially in extremes. I may say that sports aren't important, but my actions will contradict my words if I spend every Sunday afternoon glued to the televised game of the day.

And we communicate our values by how we spend our money. My father-in-law was determined that his son and daughter graduate from college. He sacrificed and saved so that his dream could become a reality. Education was valuable to Dad.

All of these examples involve observable actions and reactions. Children especially are influenced by role models (parents, teachers, older kids, sports heroes, ministers, and others they look up to). They take it all in—and learn.

Now think for a moment. What kind of role models would you like *your* children to have? What kind of values would you like these adults to portray? I would like my kids to see people who "walk" their "talk," living out biblical values.

A short list of biblical values would include:
- loving God with all our hearts (Luke 10:27);
- loving our neighbors as ourselves (Luke 10:27);
- making Christ the center of our lives (Matthew 6:33);
- loving our families (Ephesians 6:1-4);
- caring for those in need (Matthew 25:31-46);
- loving our brothers and sisters in Christ (John 13:34-35);
- reading, studying, and applying God's Word (2 Timothy 2:15);
- praying (Ephesians 6:18).

I'm sure you can add to this list.

As Christians and as Christian ministers, these values should be reflected in where we give our attention, how we spend our time, and where we invest our resources.

My point is simply this: We who lead, teach, and counsel young people wield tremendous influence by our lifestyles. Kids look up to us, and whether or not they realize it, they copy how we live. A vital part of the ministry is modeling values.

And it doesn't matter if you are only with some kids for an hour or so a week. What they see in you can still influence them. At the very least you can reinforce the positive values that others are modeling.

Treating young people with respect and love; accepting and affirming individuals; playing fair; doing the assignments yourself that you give the class; taking an active role in church; going out of your way to see kids or to drop them notes and cards; speaking out against what you believe is wrong—all of these actions model Christian values.

But we've touched on all that before. The heart of this chapter is the last half of the phrase, "Model values and teach skills." So let's look at what it means to teach skills.

TEACH SKILLS

With Webster's help, we have seen that a skill is a proficiency, the ability to do something well. When this term is used, doctors, musicians, craftsmen, or technicians usually come to mind. If we say a surgeon is "highly skilled," we mean that she is at the top of her profession. But skills are important in every area of life, and the most important of these are basic "life skills."

"We should train junior highers in basic skills that they'll need for adulthood. Emerging adults need to learn how to make good decisions, how to take responsibility, how to communicate with others. In the past, adolescents became apprentices to adults who taught them skills that prepared them for adulthood. Today the only skills many adolescents learn are playing video games, watching television, listening to rock music, and surviving on junk food. Unfortunately, these skills are of only questionable use in adulthood."

From "Focus on Junior High" by Wayne Rice, *Youthworker Journal,* Spring 1988.

Simply defined, a life skill is the ability to perform well a life-related task. Life skills would include how to make friends, how to communicate effectively, how to be a good friend, how to make a decision, how to take care of yourself, how to solve problems, and many others.

As adults, we take most of these skills for granted, but we learned them at some time in our lives. And the time that they should be learned is in early adolescence. We have already discussed the fact that children at this age are working on developing competency (see chapter 2). They want to be able to do things adequately, to accomplish something, to be good, to learn "how to." At the same time, they are in transition physically, emotionally, intellectually, spiritually, and socially. They are moving toward becoming independent and living on their own in the world, so they desperately need to learn how to relate and how to function in society.

Parents and others often assume that children will learn life skills by watching Mom and Dad in action—that these skills can be caught through modeling. But as important as modeling is for inculcating values, it doesn't work for learning skills. Skills must be taught.

Suppose you want your child to learn how to tie his shoelaces. He can watch you tie your shoes day after day, for weeks. He will know that tying shoes is important to you. But he still won't know how to do it himself until you teach him.

That's a simple example—tying shoes is not a crucial skill to miss. And eventually he will learn from you or from someone else, or he will wear slip-ons the rest of his life. But there are important life skills that he should learn. In fact, most social

---

Social Competency

"One of the important components in preventing adolescent chemical abuse is social competency. A number of social skills, all of which can be promoted by family, school, church, or other organizations, can serve as important factors in prevention. These include friendship-making skills, communication skills, decision-making skills, and the ability to say 'no' when peer pressure mounts."

Dr. Peter L. Benson, president of the Search Institute, from "Source," a newsletter on youth and family published by Search Institute.

scientists agree that the absence of life skills can be devastating to children and one of the leading causes of delinquency and crime. They also agree that the best time to teach life skills is during early adolescence.

As we minister to junior high young people, we can help meet this pressing need. Consider teaching life skills as a part of your junior high ministry.

Teaching any skill involves four steps: explanation, demonstration, supervised practice with feedback, and independent practice in a real life setting.

If I were teaching you how to use an electric lawn edger, first I would explain how the edger works, pointing out the blade, guide, cord, switch, and other important parts. I would also explain how to hold the edger and how to place it next to the lawn and operate it. That's "explanation."

Next, I would demonstrate the equipment for you. After unwrapping the extension cord and plugging it in, I would place the edger between the lawn and sidewalk. Then I would press the switch and push the edger a few feet, while carefully explaining what is happening. Afterward, I would ask if you had any questions.

In the third step, "supervised practice," I would give you the tool and let you try it yourself, under my watchful eye. As you edged a few feet of lawn, I would make sure you did it right, making corrections and answering any questions you might have about the operation of the equipment.

For the final step, you would be on your own. I would give you the edger so that you could edge your own lawn. But before you left, I would encourage you to call if you needed help.

That's how to teach skills—explanation, demonstration, supervised practice, and independent practice. But how does this relate to junior high ministry? Let's expand these steps to show how they would fit into a youth meeting.

1. *Objective: What do you want students to learn?*
Divide the larger skill into bite-sized pieces—then write a concise and measurable goal for the meeting. For example, the life skill "How to handle emotions" could be broken down into: recogniz-

ing emotional clues, describing feelings during difficult times, identifying contributing causes for feelings, and reacting to intense feelings. "How to manage money" could be divided into: getting more
money without depending on gifts, dividing money (simple bud-
geting), designing a spending plan, avoiding impulse buying, and
shopping to get the best value for the money.

As you begin to teach the skill, simply tell students what you are
going to teach them. State what you would like to see happen as a
result of the time together. In a meeting about not smoking, drinking,
and using drugs, you could say: "As a result of this meeting, you will
choose to stay away from the power stealers—alcohol, cigarettes, and
drugs. Our goal is that you will choose life."

You don't always have to give the objective, but saying it helps
everyone understand where the meeting is going.

2. Set: Why do the learners need to learn this?

When you came to me and asked to borrow my lawn edger, you
already knew that you had a need. You were ready to learn. Kids,
however, often have no idea that they need to learn certain life
skills. They may sense that something is wrong, but seldom will
they identify the reason. It is important, therefore, to set the stage
for the teaching by getting students ready to learn.

This can be done by explaining why the material is important,
presenting the advantages of learning it, and relating the material to
life experiences at school, church, or home.

A series of questions, a game, case studies, role plays, or other
discussion starters can be very effective. In "Set," you help students see and feel problem so that they will want to find the
solution.

3. Delivery: What content do I want them to learn? How will I teach this content?

For this step, select the material to be taught and the appropriate
teaching approach. Then teach toward your objective, using creative methods. This is the "explanation" step we discussed earlier.
Having presented the problem in "Set," you are now giving the
solution.

Suppose you wanted to teach kids where to find friends—that was your objective. For "Set," you could have them list the first names of all their friends. Then, looking at their cards, they could think about whether or not there is anyone on the list with whom they would like to be very good friends. Next, you could tell them a story about a boy who just moved to a new town and had no friends. Afterward, you could say that probably, at times, all of us have felt lonely, like that boy. We wanted friends but didn't know where to find them. Then you could explain that as a result of this meeting, they will know where to find potential friends.

Because of "Set," your students would be ready to hear what you have to say. They would be ready for "Delivery." Be creative and concise in this section. Make the point and give them a way to remember it. I have found that acronyms work well. For example, to resolve conflicts at home, just remember CLASP: C = calm down; L = lower your voice; A = acknowledge the other person's request; S = state your request; and P = propose a solution.

Physical objects can also be effective. For the lesson on conflict resolution, we gave everyone a metal clasp to keep in the pocket as a reminder of our acronym.

4. *Demonstration: How can I show them what I mean?*
Don't just talk about it; give concrete examples. Anyone can demonstrate the concept or skill you are trying to get across, including the leader, another volunteer, or other students.

As in our edger story, this step means giving a living example of what you have just taught. Consider the lesson on resolving conflict. As the teacher, I could demonstrate CLASP by role playing with another staff member a typical fight between siblings, working through CLASP one step at a time. Afterward, I could have kids point out what I did to "acknowledge his request," etc. Then we could act out another situation. It is important for students to see the skill in action.

5. *Check: Is the content and process at the correct level of difficulty?*

This means making sure the learners understand the material. You can use a variety of monitoring devices such as raised hands, discussion, sharing with a neighbor, or comment cards. Use "Check" throughout the teaching session.

6. *Practice: How can I let them try it?*
Learning + Practice = Retention. Give students an opportunity to practice, with immediate feedback and reinforcements. With some skills, this will be easy because they can do everything they should right in the room. If you were teaching them how to start a conversation, they could divide into pairs and start conversations using the method you just taught them.

Some skills do not lend themselves to physical practice in a meeting (e.g., finding friends, reacting to a crisis, shopping, studying, etc.). But students can still practice by thinking through what they would do in certain situations, by role playing, or by responding to case studies.

Whatever the skill, young people need the opportunity to practice under your supervision.

7. *Action: How can I help them apply this to their lives?*
This is independent practice, an assignment for students to carry out in the next week.

Summarize, give opportunity for questions and comments, and then tell them what to do during the days that follow. Have kids report to someone during the week or at the beginning of your next meeting. The assignment is not complete until they report back.

Here are some examples of action assignments:
● This week, meet three new people.
● This week, check and double-check your work on every test you take at school.
● This week, do one of the actions you wrote on your card for improving your family times.
● Use one of these compliments when you get home, and all three during the week.
● This week, read the Bible for about five minutes every day.

Life Skills Evaluation			
	Beginning 1 2	Intermediate 3 4	Advanced 5
Prayer	Talks to God when in trouble	Prays for own self	Has prayer list
Bible Study	Reads the Bible occasionally	Knows how to have devotions	Has a regular Bible study
Church Atten-dance	Chooses, attends, finds friends at church	Attends church & youth group regularly	Worship Sacraments Small group
Lan-guage	Before swearing, counts to 10	Makes positive comments, reduces swearing	Encourages others
Phys-ical Care	No drugs Begins personal hygiene	No smoking or addictions	Improves dress, hygiene, diet, and exercise
Prob-lem Solving	Recognizes problems, chooses alter- natives	Understands lord- ship of Christ	Uses "Stop, Look, Listen, Go" to solve problems
Spir-itual Growth	Recognizes areas of need	Seeks Christ's attitude; balanced life	Sets goals for personal growth
Love Toward Others	Stops resenting others	Understands Golden Rule; shows kindness	Makes sacrifices for others

by Dwight Spotts, Executive Director of Spokane Youth for Christ.

As you plan meetings for teaching life skills, remember objective, set, delivery, demonstration, check, practice, and action. In Youth for Christ's Campus Life/JV program, these elements are organized into the following format.

OPENER (5 minutes)—a game or activity designed for fun and to help everyone relax and get into the meeting. The openers are not too rowdy but involve everyone and are active.

ANNOUNCEMENTS (5 minutes)—another game or creative presentation to promote upcoming events and highlight special occasions within the group (e.g., special awards, birthdays, etc.).

STARTERS (5 minutes)—activities designed to set the stage for the teaching, helping the young people think about the topic that will be taught. Typical starters are quizzes, role plays, skits, case studies, stories, etc.

TELL (5 minutes)—the "delivery" segment where the life skill is taught.

"Outward appearances can be deceiving. A mature looking thirteen-year-old may be very immature. So don't be surprised when kids act their age (or younger). You can't always tell what they're like by looking at their physical development. Too often youth workers assume that the 'more mature' kids don't need the basics or personal attention, when, in fact, they may need it more.

"This also highlights the need for a team approach to the ministry, so that individual attention may be given where needed."

Richard Dunn, Chairman of the Department of Youth Ministry, Trinity College (Deerfield, Illinois).

SHOW (5 minutes)—the segment where the life skill is demonstrated.

DO (10 minutes)—an activity designed to reinforce the main point of the teaching by having young people practice what they have just been taught.

THOUGHT FOR THE WEEK (5 minutes)—a Bible lesson designed to build a foundation of biblical knowledge so students can make responsible and thoughtful decisions for Christ.

THE BIGGIE (5 minutes) — a meeting-ending game or activity to give everyone something to look forward to and to give them something to talk about at school the next day. It usually involves competition between individuals, team representatives, or small groups.

You may organize your meeting differently by adding games or music. Just be sure to include the teaching elements.

Besides the life skills that I listed earlier, there are other skills which Christian young people need to learn. These include: how to pray, how to study the Bible, how to worship, how to serve others, how to share the faith, and so forth. Consider teaching these skills when you design Sunday School or other Christian education programs. We will discuss how to study the Bible in the next chapter.

Because early adolescents are at the crossroads and are working on competency, they need to learn life skills. Model values and teach them skills.

(By the way, can I have my edger back?)

(Note: Many of the examples in this chapter were taken from *Campus Life/JV, Year 1, Year 2, and Year 3.*)

THINK IT THROUGH

1. What values do kids see modeled by the way you teach and relate to them?

2. From your observations of junior high kids, why is it important for them to learn life skills?

3. What life skills do the kids in your youth group need to learn?

4. What program do you have in place where you could teach life skills?

5. Who would be the teacher?

6. What "spiritual life skills" do your kids need to learn?

CHAPTER 10

ROUTE 66

The teacher stood and read from the book:

"And it came to pass, verily, that she seemeth amongst
and in the midst, that he sayeth unto her, 'Yea and
wouldest thou that whatever he wilt shalt be done
according to whowhatwhensoever Ezracharophis,
begotten of Zedopariah from the land beyond
Berithamah cometh?'
"Insomuch as the woman knew not the messenger nor
his wondrous companions shining all about the company,
and yet she remaineth silent, looking for the sign nor the
seal betwixt the eyes. And the whole of the congregation
around the candlestick riseth with loud praisulations
according to the prophetic word.
From Hesitations 14:37a."

If you found that incomprehensible, consider your poor
junior highers. That's how the Bible sounds to many of
them—a string of adult words and empty gibberish.
For the unchurched, the Bible is just an old book.

There may be one at home, on a shelf or coffee table, but it is seldom opened. Most have very little idea of what is inside the dusty covers although they may have heard the Bible read or quoted occasionally. They are biblically illiterate.

Even kids who have grown up in church aren't sure what the Bible teaches. Some may know certain facts or some of the classic Bible stories but probably don't have the slightest idea how the stories relate to today and to their lives.

"The whole Bible was given to us by inspiration from God and is useful to teach us what is true and to make us realize what is wrong in our lives; it straightens us out and helps us do what is right. It is God's way of making us well prepared at every point, fully equipped to do good to everyone" (2 Timothy 3:16-17, TLB).

The Bible is God's Word, and kids need to know what it says and teaches. As people concerned about junior highers, we must teach them this invaluable life skill—how to study the Bible.

PRACTICING WHAT WE PREACH

Before we teach them, however, we should be students of the Word ourselves. This means being disciplined in our Bible study habits—reading, understanding, and applying Scripture.

Do you really believe that the Bible is God's inspired Word? If so, you will read the Bible.

Why People Don't Read Their Bibles

1. Perception of irrelevance
2. Lack of accountability
3. Poor study habits
4. Difficulty of interpretation
5. Noise (interruptions and busy schedules)
6. Resistance to change

As reported by the Barna Research Group and Dr. Bruce Barton of The Livingstone Corporation.

Do you really believe that biblical principles are relevant for today? If so, you will study the Bible.

Do you really believe that God speaks to us through His Word? If so, you will apply the Bible to your life.

Do you really believe that God knows what is best for you? If so, you will obey what He tells you through the Bible.

Take an honest look at your own Bible study habits before challenging others to read Scripture and trying to teach them how.

SETTING THE STAGE

One of the mistakes often made by Christian youth workers is to jump right in with a spiritual agenda, assuming that young people want to learn about God. Most kids are more concerned with grades, physical changes, social pressures, and feelings of failure. And besides, why should they be interested in that ancient, dry, and difficult book?

Before teaching, we must set the stage for learning.

Create Thirst

A thirsty person will readily accept an offer of a drink. In fact, he will do almost anything to satisfy his need. Unlike thirst for water, however, Bible reading is not a felt need. In fact, most kids at this age think they are doing fine on their own, without the Bible. So we must create a thirst—motivate them. We want kids to WANT to read, understand, and apply God's Word.

How you create this thirst, of course, will depend on the make-up of your group. Strangers to Christianity should be handled differently than VBS veterans. But here are some suggestions:

● Use biblical examples in your teaching and conversation. We covered this briefly in chapter 7. No matter what the subject, you can probably find a Bible story or quote to illustrate your point.

"Speaking of running away—remember what happened to Jonah? God wanted him to go one way, but he went the opposite. Eventually Jonah was swallowed by a huge fish—and lived to tell about it. (But that's another story.) Anyway, when we run away from our problems, we usually run into worse ones!"

"If you ever feel lonely and depressed, just remember Elijah. You may have heard of him. Elijah was a prophet who. . . ."

"Talk about loyalty, Ruth was as loyal as you can get. She left her homeland, friends, and family and went with her mother-in-law, of all people! (Eventually she even had a book of the Bible written about her.)"

By hearing stories like these, kids will build their biblical knowledge and their curiosity. They will want to read more about the exciting characters and learn more about what's in the Book.

Don't carry this to an extreme; but sprinkling your teaching with Bible stories and examples, in a natural way, will help create interest in reading the Bible.

● Give examples of how you and others have applied God's Word. Again, this can be very effective, but it must be natural, not forced.

Imagine you are talking with a few kids about summer vacation plans. You mention the fact that during family devotions (a regular time of reading and discussing the Bible), you read a verse that helped you make a decision. This casual comment can plant the thought that the Bible is a source of guidance.

Or if while explaining how you coped with a personal tragedy, you share how certain verses meant so much during that difficult time. Kids would begin to see that the Bible can be a source of comfort.

Or during a discussion about "love," you tell them about the love chapter (1 Corinthians 13). They would start to understand that the Bible can be a source of answers for their questions about life.

When kids see what the Bible does for you, they will want to know more about it for themselves.

● Use physical reminders. Schoolteachers often pepper their walls with quotes, pictures, and posters, so your kids won't find it unusual for you to put a Bible verse on the wall. Christian bookstores have a fine selection of beautiful posters with Scripture references or whole verses printed on them. You can also play Christian music tapes from time to time. And, of course, you can have your Bible with you in the car and in the room.

These visual statements can reinforce the fact that the Bible is important to you and should be important to them as well.

Provide Tools
If possible, whenever you read the Bible with kids, whether it's in Sunday School, at youth group, or on a retreat, make sure that everyone has access to a copy of what you are reading.

In a small group, you can have Bibles for everyone. When the "Reach Out" edition of *The Living Bible* first came out, I used to have a box of them in my trunk. Although our Campus Life "Insight" meetings featured discussions on Christian growth and Bible study, most of the kids didn't own Bibles; or if they did, they would forget to bring them. And so they would use the ones I brought. No one felt out of place, and everyone could participate. Even now, in our Sunday School program, we will bring several of the church Bibles to the classroom. Although all the students in that class own several Bibles, they usually forget to bring them to church.

In larger groups, students could pair up, or you could use an overhead projector and put the passage on the screen.

Also, it is important to use an understandable translation of the Bible. Don't allow archaic or adult words to become a barrier. There are several fine versions available.

Remove Barriers
Some people avoid the Bible because it looks and feels strange to them. That's not surprising, considering the fact that the Bible is organized like no other book they've ever seen—with sixty-six smaller books, hundreds of chapters, and thousands of numbered verses. And most kids don't know the order of the Bible books. Imagine what they think when asked to turn to Titus or Haggai.

One way to remove this barrier would be to have everyone use the same edition of the Bible and give page numbers when you refer to specific passages. You could post a list of all sixty-six books on the wall (on a piece of poster board). This would also help them learn the order.

Another barrier to Bible reading is knowing where to read. Often I've heard of people who, after deciding to read the Bible, approach it like any other book and begin reading at page 1. They usually stop somewhere in Leviticus. Even those who decide to start with the New Testament get bogged down in the Gospels while reading the same story over and over.

Kids need guidance in reading the Bible, especially on their own. Mark is a good place to start. It's short, action-packed, and tells the story of Jesus. James is also good because the lessons are obvious and practical. Or you could give them a series of passages to read on an interesting subject like love, family, the future, Satan, friends, etc.

Don't let barriers stand between kids and the Bible.

Dispel Fears

Kids aren't "afraid" of the Bible itself, but they are deathly afraid of being embarrassed in front of their peers. Many junior highers have trouble reading, especially reading aloud. They can imagine nothing more embarrassing than to stumble over a word and have everyone laugh. I'm not saying you should never have kids read aloud in your meetings. On the contrary—this can be an affirming and confidence-bolstering experience if handled correctly.

For reading the Bible in a group, you can dispel kids' fears by:
- preparing them for reading aloud—print out the passages you want them to read and give them time to practice.
- setting them up for success—explain to the class that it's not easy to read the Bible aloud because of the small print and difficult words, but they should just do the best they can.
- allowing no one to ridicule anyone else.
- affirming kids after they read—compliment them and thank them for helping.
- allowing them to decline—simply explain that each person can read a couple of verses (along the rows or around the circle), but they can pass if they don't want to read at this time.
- allowing them to stop and ask how to pronounce any word.

We can set the stage for Bible teaching by creating thirst, providing tools, removing barriers, and dispelling fears.

Choosing Curriculum

When choosing curriculum for your Sunday School, youth group, or other continuing program, ask the following questions:

1. Is it consistent with our goals? Make sure it takes kids in the direction you want.

2. Is it realistic? Watch out for any material that purports to take kids through the Bible in a month, bring instant maturity, develop deep disciples, or some other fantastic claim.

3. Is it simple (volunteer friendly)? In other words, can your teachers prepare and teach the lessons easily without using most of their preparation time trying to figure them out and collecting props.

4. Is it focused? Beware of material that goes in three or four directions at the same time.

5. Is it active? You don't want kids just sitting and listening to the teacher talk.

6. Is it varied and balanced?

Don't be fooled by the creative advertisements, neat packages, inexpensive price tags and bells and whistles. Open it up and read through actual lesson plans to choose curriculum that is right for you and your group.

TEACHING THEM HOW

Most Bible study methods have three main steps: read, understand, and apply. Readers are told to answer these questions about a passage: "What does it say?" "What does it mean?" and "How do I apply it?" But early adolescents need these steps simplified and explained in concrete terms.

It is also important to start small—choose a paragraph or short story to read and study, not a whole chapter or book.

And kids need to see how the Bible is up-to-date and practical, so use contemporary illustrations and applications.

I have found a five-step Bible study process to be quite effective. The steps are easy to teach and to remember. And what's more important, they answer the questions "So what?" ("What does that passage have to do with me?") and "Now what?" ("What should I do about it?") Use this process to teach the Bible and *teach* this process to your kids so that they will be able to study the Bible for themselves.

When you teach this Bible study method, don't give it to them all at once. Instead, help them master one step at a time. Because each step builds on the previous ones, you will be able to review them as you go along.

Also, be sure to use many junior high illustrations for each step, especially "present" and "plan."

These steps can be seen on the chart below.

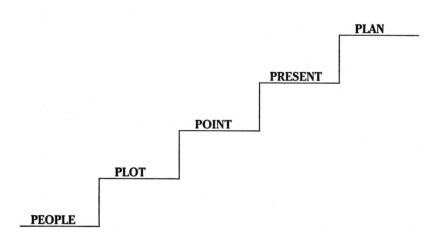

Let's consider these steps, one at a time.

People
The first step in reading and understanding a Bible passage is to identify the *people* involved. This is a good first step for junior highers because it is easy and concrete. And later it will help them see themselves in the story.

The people can be those who are mentioned by name or role, those who are hearing the story, the storyteller or writer, and anyone else connected with the passage.

Mark 1:1-4 (TLB) says: "Here begins the wonderful story of Jesus the Messiah, the Son of God. In the book written by the prophet Isaiah, God announced that He would send His Son to earth, and that a special messenger would arrive first to prepare the world for His coming. 'This messenger will live out in the barren wilderness,' Isaiah said, 'and will proclaim that everyone must straighten out his life to be ready for the Lord's arrival.' This messenger was John the Baptist. He lived in the wilderness and taught that all should be baptized as a public announcement of their decision to turn their backs on sin, so that God could forgive them."

A complete list of the people in this story would include: Jesus, Isaiah, God, John the Baptist, the people who heard John speak, "everyone," and Mark, the writer. As you can see, by including the writer and the readers or listeners, every story in the Bible has people to identify. This is an important first step and one that every junior higher can do. It answers the question "Who?"

At this point, you may also want to ask, "Where do you see yourself in the story? Which person are you most like?" In Mark 1:16-20, Jesus calls some fishermen to be His disciples. Besides Mark, the people in the story are Jesus, Simon, Andrew, James, John, Zebedee, and the hired men. You could describe the personalities of the fishermen and then ask which one they think they are most like. Obviously, this question will be much easier to answer in some passages (e.g., historical narratives) than in others; but with any passage, it will help kids put the Bible into a contemporary setting.

Plot
Next we move to *plot*. This step answers the questions "Where?" and "What?" and helps students understand what the passage is all about.

At this point you should explain about context—that the surrounding verses and chapters can help if the specific passage doesn't contain the answers.

In the Mark 1:1-4 example, the answer to "Where is this taking place?" (for the main thrust of the passage) is: the Judean wilderness. And the answer to "What is happening?" is: John the Baptist is telling everyone to be ready for the Lord's arrival by turning away from sin.

Notice that the answers for "people" and "plot" are very simple and straightforward. No one should be looking for deep, hidden meanings in the text. In effect, we are answering the question, "What does the text say?" These steps help kids understand what was going on back then. Everyone in your group should be able to climb these first two steps.

Point

This is a more difficult step, but it is a crucial one for understanding and applying the Bible. Here you will be helping young people discover the biblical principle, the timeless truth, of the passage.

Explain that the *point* of a passage is simply the lesson or moral of the story. To discover the point, your young people need only to ask and answer one of two questions: "What is God like?" or "What should people be like?" In other words, every Bible story will either tell us something about God and what He is like, or something about people and what they should be like—how they should live. And sometimes the story will tell us both.

Returning to Mark 1:1-4, we could conclude that the point of the story is that God's plan is for people to turn from their sins in order to be ready to receive the Lord.

Let's look at another passage in Mark. In chapter 3, verses 1-6, we read about Jesus healing a man with a deformed hand. The *people* in the story are: Jesus, a man with a deformed hand, the Pharisees, the congregation in the synagogue, the Herodians, and Mark, the writer of the passage.

For *plot*, we see that Jesus healed a deformed man in front of the congregation on the Sabbath in a synagogue, the Jewish house of worship, in the city of Capernaum.

For *point*, we see that this story answers both questions. It tells us what God is like because we see Jesus' anger at the Pharisees' indifference to human need and His compassion for the man with the deformed hand. But we could also say that the point of the story is that people should have pity on those in need and try to help them.

Try to state the point of the story in one sentence.

It may take some time for your kids to do this step, but make sure they learn it well. *Point* answers the question "What does the passage mean?" and is the turning point of serious Bible study.

Present

Now that we've seen what the passage says and means, we come to "How do I apply it?" This involves the last two steps in the process.

Present means putting the story and its meaning in a contemporary setting, bringing it into the here and now. The easiest way to do this is to retrace the first three steps, but bringing them into the present. Ask: "Who could these people be today?" "Where could this take place today?" (or "Where *does* this happen today?") "What would be the result, here and now?" Tell kids to use their imaginations.

For example, if Jesus came to their neighborhoods looking for disciples, who would He call, where would He go, and what would He say? And how would they respond to His call?

Then ask how they see the *point* applying to today's circumstances and problems. To help answer this question, give them the following categories: family, friends, faith, and future. Explain that the *point* of the passage will have an application in at least one of these four areas.

The point of Mark 1:1-4 is that God's plan is for people to turn from their sins in order to be ready to receive the Lord. For one person this could have an impact on her *faith* as she realizes that she should turn from her sins. Someone else might realize that this point could affect his *friends*, because he should be like John the Baptist and tell them about Christ.

The Mark 3:1-6 story could also affect faith and friends as we begin to have compassion on those in need.

Our fourth step, *present*, takes the timeless truth and makes it timely. It brings the biblical principle into daily life.

Plan

Now we come to the last step, *plan*. As mentioned earlier, this step answers the question "Now what?" It helps us decide what we are going to do to put into practice what we have learned in *point* and *present*. This is an action plan.

Unfortunately, most Bible "application" stops before this step. People think they have applied Scripture if they come up with an "ought" statement for themselves (e.g., "I ought to stop complaining"; "I ought to be nicer to my sister"; "I ought to read the Bible and pray daily" etc.). But that's not enough.

It's great to discover the biblical principle and see how it relates to our family, friends, faith, or future. But true application won't happen if we don't make a decision as to what we will actually *do* about it.

Let's say I am reading the Bible, and I become convicted about my relationship with Gail, my wife. As a result of my reading, I decide that I ought to be more loving and considerate of her. That answers "So what?" But, "Now what?" What will I do to actually put that "ought" into practice in my life? That's the crucial question.

To help kids with the *plan* step, tell them to remember three words: PRAY, LOOK, and DO. The action plan will relate to these three areas. PRAY means deciding what they can pray about. LOOK means deciding what they should look for. And DO means deciding the action they should take.

In the Mark 3:1-6 story, we saw that the *point* is that we should have compassion on those in need and try to help them. This would affect PRAY because we could ask God to open our eyes to see the needy people around us. It would also affect LOOK and DO. We should look for better ways to help those *specific* people we know who need help; and we should _____ (DO) to help them.

If I want to be more loving and considerate of my wife, my plan could include clearing the table after dinner *tonight* and taking her out to dinner this weekend. Those are specific actions—that's *plan*.

A way to illustrate how this works together is to draw the following arrow.

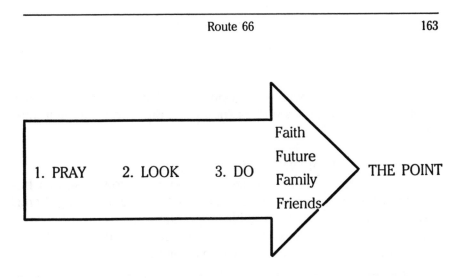

1. PRAY   2. LOOK   3. DO   Faith
                                  Future   THE POINT
                                  Family
                                  Friends

God Speaks through the Bible

"Many are content with general applications of what they read and so do not get clear guidelines from God. We must endeavor to be specific in our applications. An example of a general application is 'Christians must love their enemies.' A more specific application of this same verse is 'I must love Bob, even though he has been spreading slanderous stories about me. I am very busy today. But I will offer to take him and his child to see the doctor.'

"A second way God speaks to us is by giving us biblical principles. These are truths about topics such as what God is like and how He acts, or the nature of man, the world, heaven, hell, or the Christian life. Here God is like a teacher who presents important facts in a classroom. These facts may not have an immediate application to our lives, but we still need to take them and hide them in our hearts (Psalm 119:11). In this way we fill up a reservoir of truth in our hearts that can be tapped when the need arises."

Ajith Fernando, National Director of Youth for Christ/Sri Lanka, from an article in *Practical Christianity* (Wheaton, Ill.: Tyndale House Publishers, 1987).

To *plan* means to decide what God wants us to pray, look, and do (and then do it). That's understanding the Bible and putting it into practice in our lives.

HOLDING THEM ACCOUNTABLE
As in teaching any life skill (see chapter 9), students should be given assignments and then be held accountable for doing them. This is very important for Bible application. Think of what you could have kids do, away from the meeting, to help them get into the Bible and put it into practice in their lives.

> "We've found that kids do well when we've given them a little more ownership of the process. We have notebooks with our logo on the front. We photocopy assignments and have kids keep them in the notebooks. (The notebooks are theirs to keep.) Occasionally we do special events that are 'notebooks only'—only those caught up on their work may come."
>
> Gregg Lafferty, Junior High Minister of Wheaton Bible Church (Wheaton, Illinois).

You could have them rewrite a chapter in their own words, read for five minutes a day, fill out a "people-plot-point-present-plan" sheet for a passage, memorize a verse, explain the meaning of a story to a parent or a friend, carry out the action step in *plan*, or another similar assignment.

These assignments will give them the opportunity for independent practice and will reinforce what they learned in the class.

When you give these assignments, however, be sure to check on how they did at your next meeting or before. You (or another staff member) could give them a call; you could assign "buddies"; you could have a regular check-up time in each meeting.

To make sure that kids learn to study and apply the Bible, follow up on your assignments to hold kids accountable.

There are 100,000,000 Bibles in this country, but few people read or study them. Studying the Bible is a value and a skill that most kids will not learn on their own. You can help transform lives by teaching kids how to study the Bible and apply it. It is God's way of making us well prepared at every point, fully equipped to do good to everyone.

(The "People, Plot, Point, Present, Plan" Bible Study pattern is adapted from Youth for Christ's "Campus Life/JV—Year One." Used by permission.)

THINK IT THROUGH

1. Why do you think it is important for kids to learn how to study the Bible?

2. When do *you* read and study the Bible? What Bible study method do you use?

3. What does it mean to apply the Bible?

4. Who in your group would be receptive to beginning a program of personal Bible study?

5. When would be the best time and place to teach your kids how to study the Bible?

6. What could you do to help motivate your kids to study the Bible?

7. What will you do to hold kids accountable for their Bible study assignments?

CHAPTER 11

SPITBALLS AND PITFALLS

What has twenty-four arms, twenty-four legs, and twelve
heads, moves constantly, and can eat you alive? The
answer: twelve junior high kids.

Perhaps the most terrifying prospect for any potential
youth worker is facing a roomful of kids out of control.
And let's face it — even one junior higher
can be a monster!

- Kevin is a seventh-grader with a high school body. The
biggest kid in the group, he bullies everyone and insists on
his own way. And during Sunday School, Kevin constantly
disrupts by picking on a couple of the sixth-graders.

- Shyness has never been a problem for Jennifer. In fact,
her mouth seems to be in perpetual motion as she talks
about boys, school, boys, the party last night, boys, and
anything else that comes up (did I mention boys?). And it
doesn't matter where she is — youth group, concert,
Sunday School, worship — Jenny and friends talk,
whisper, and pass notes.

- Everyone knows what Matt will say—something gross or dirty. In every crowdbreaker, discussion, or conversation, he finds a way to talk about the bathroom, sex, or other assorted bodily functions.
- Tanya and Paul are into cutting and throwing. Any worksheet, pencil, or miscellaneous debris in their hands quickly becomes a missile to be hurled at a victim across the room.
- Competitive is an apt description of Dave. Everything's a game, and he has to win. And so Dave yells, argues, and even cheats to be victorious.

How many Kevins, Jennifers, Matts, Tanyas, Pauls, and Daves do you know? I'm sure you could add many of your own case studies of colorful personalities. Any one of them can disrupt a meeting and even throw it into chaos. And sometimes all of them will be in one youth group!

Let's face it, "junior high" and "energy" are synonymous—interruptions and disruptions are occupational hazards for anyone working with kids this age. So if you want to get through to them, you will have to know how to channel their energy and keep it under control.

WHAT IS DISCIPLINE?

Often the word "discipline" evokes pictures of drill sergeants, tough coaches, mean teachers, or stern parents. Discipline is seen as punishment for stepping out of line or breaking the rules. It is negative.

But the basic meaning of "discipline" is positive. Coming from the word "disciple" which means a learner or follower, discipline means organizing, training, and guiding toward a goal. A runner preparing for a marathon works diligently for three months, increasing his mileage each week until he is ready for the race. He is disciplined. A concert pianist practices for hours each day to perfect her technique. She is disciplined. A salesman organizes his day and forces himself to make a certain number of calls. He is disciplined.

Discipline is important in every area of life, including youth ministry. We need to be self-disciplined, controlling ourselves and using well our time and other resources. And we should help kids become disciplined, moving them toward maturity. If you see discipline as necessary and positive action to help the ministry, you won't back away from doing what you should.

1. *Discipline is educational*

Little babies cry whenever they need anything, no matter where they are—in church, in a restaurant, or in the presence of the Pope—and regardless of how their screams affect others. As children grow and mature, they learn (hopefully) that there are more acceptable forms of expression. In Ecclesiastes we read that there is a time for everything under heaven. Kids need to know that they can't do whatever they want, whenever they want. Discipline will teach them that fact of life.

Discipline

"Discipline and instruction go hand in hand. Teaching without discipline is an impossible task. The outcome of discipline should not be anger but rather an attitude of learning and correction of the behavior so that the child benefits. The following four principles apply to discipline.
1. The goal of discipline should be to build self-control and responsibility.
2. The dignity of the child should be preserved throughout the process.
3. Discipline methods need to promote a positive learning climate.
4. Private correction is usually preferable and more effective than public rebuke."

From "Follow Me" by Tom Sawyer, Fall 1987.

Freud said that maturity is the ability to postpone gratification. That's another lesson for kids to learn—sometimes they have to wait. And they need to learn that their actions lead to certain consequences. They can't do anything they want and get away with it.

The teacher who insists on order instead of chaos in the class-room, the parent who makes sure that children share instead of acting selfishly, the coach who enforces the rules of the game and doesn't allow cheating, and the youth leader who won't let one person spoil an activity for everyone else all give young people invaluable lessons. Discipline teaches.

2. *Discipline is practical*
Exercising crowd control just makes sense. That's why there are ushers, security guards, and police officers at professional sporting events. What would a junior high meeting be like with no guide-lines, rules, or order? Some of the kids might have fun, but very little would be accomplished. There must be rules for the smooth running of the meeting or activity and for effective communication. If you want your event to meet your objective, you will need discipline.

3. *Discipline is responsible*
Working with young people is serious business. After all, each one is someone's child, a valuable creation of a loving God, and must be handled with care. Although kids may resent rules, thinking that they hinder freedom, most regulations are imposed for physical and emotional protection.

I'm sure these rules and guidelines sound familiar: "No standing in front of this line on the bus"; "No running on the pool deck"; "Look both ways before crossing the street"; "Don't run while holding an open pair of scissors." As the person in charge of these young lives, you are responsible for their safety.

Fresh out of college and into youth ministry, I couldn't wait for high school camp, thinking it would be great being the counselor and "buddy" to the guys in the cabin. I wanted to get to know them and be their friend. And so I was reluctant to be the "hard guy" and enforce rules like the 11 P.M. curfew and "lights out." Instead, I laughed and wrestled with them before pulling my sleeping bag over my head just after midnight. The rest of that first night was a mess, as cereal, shaving cream, and toilet paper flew around the room. I tried to reason with them, but no one would listen. Finally, I left and slept elsewhere.

I know that sounds crazy, but I was afraid of alienating the guys, so I let them walk all over me. They almost destroyed the cabin in the process. Another summer, a young man almost died from a fall from an upper bunk during a pillow fight.

During those early camping experiences, I remember listening to the camp director spell out the rules at our first meeting—"no alcoholic beverages, no guys in girls' cabins or vice versa, . . ."—and I thought: "I'm glad he's doing that and not me. I don't want to be seen as the bad guy, the policeman."

But after a few dozen camps, retreats, and trips, and experiences like those above, my opinion had changed 180 degrees. I even volunteered to give the "rules speech." What made the difference? I realized my responsibility as their leader and how important those rules were for everyone's safety.

As a responsible youth leader, you will need to explain and enforce certain rules.

WHAT DO KIDS EXPECT?

In that initial camp experience, I made the mistake common to many youth leaders—I assumed that kids are turned off by anyone exercising authority and telling them what to do. But I found the opposite to be true. They expect adults to act like adults—that includes guiding and directing them.

Some youth workers are intimidated by the kids, thinking: "Why would they listen to me and do what I say?" But remember what we covered in chapter 6—usually junior highers will respect and even obey you because of your position and because you are an adult. I'm not saying that discipline will be a piece of cake. There will be times when you may have to ask a disruptive person to leave or call his parents. But don't let the kids intimidate you. Even a large crowd of junior highers can be controlled by a person who speaks firmly and authoritatively and then backs up his or her words with actions.

Junior high kids, especially, need and want adult supervision. Although they will test the limits constantly, having those limits gives them a sense of security. They know that someone is in charge and that someone cares.

Kids don't want or need an endless list of rules and someone to tell them what to do every inch of their lives. But the other extreme, no limits and total freedom, is scary, and they can't handle it.

We'll cover *how* to discipline in a minute, but for now, just know that being the disciplinarian will not hurt your ministry with kids. Don't be afraid to step up to the challenge and step in to do what you must—to keep order, keep on track, and move kids toward maturity. They expect it.

THE PROPER CLIMATE

Effective discipline takes place in a positive climate of acceptance and affirmation. If kids know that you care about them, they will be more open to your correction and guidance.

Acceptance

Accepting someone for who she is does not mean that you approve of everything she does. But your acceptance of that person will build her self-esteem and your relationship with her. Consider how God relates to us. Throughout Scripture we see evidence of God's love and acceptance, even though we ignore and disobey Him. We don't have to dress up for God or become like someone else, but we do have to repent, turning from our sin and turning to Christ. God hates the sin but loves the sinner.

Accept kids as they really are, with all their imperfections, not expecting them to be beautiful, talented, and intelligent. Then help them see the error of their ways and guide them in the right direction.

Affirmation

Look for ways to affirm kids, complimenting them on what they do that is right. Discipline involves guiding and teaching. If they're already headed the right way, encourage them to keep going.

Maturity
Remember, you are an adult, so act like one. If kids break the rules, act up, or even defy your authority, don't take it personally. Even if their attacks are meant to be personal, don't let them throw you off course. The quickest way to lose kids is to lose your cool. You can get them to do almost anything, but if you yell at them, call them names, or use sarcasm, they will turn you off. It's not that you should never be angry with an individual or group. Just be careful how you express your anger. Cutting a person down to size with a caustic remark or snide comment will only hurt the ministry with him and with everyone watching and listening.

Humor
Although your ministry goals are serious, don't take them—or yourself—too seriously. In other words, lighten up and laugh with the kids. There is a time for enforcing rules, but there is also a time for joking and kidding around. Don't *always* be somber and serious. Let your kids see the fun side of your personality. Notice that I recommended laughing *with* kids, not at them. There's a world of difference.

Acceptance, affirmation, maturity, and humor will provide a positive climate for effective discipline.

HOW TO DISCIPLINE
Establish Boundaries
Before wading into a discipline situation, think about what boundaries you want to set—what *is not* permissible behavior. Then consider what you will allow—what *is* permissible behavior. You must answer these questions completely for yourself. Then you and your staff should agree about what is and what is not acceptable.

As you discuss the expectations and rules together, keep in mind the age and development of the kids. Some movement and noise are inevitable with junior highers. There have to be times when you let them act their age.

Consider your objectives, the kids, and your tolerance level when you establish your boundaries.

Follow-Through

"Do what you say you are going to do. This is where volunteer staff often really fall short. Junior highers can make you feel like dirt. You will think they hate you and they are no longer your friends. IMPORTANT NOTE! Junior highers bounce back unbelievably quick. Your staff needs to establish the fact that they are more than just big brothers or sisters—they are also authority figures in their lives. If this does not happen, your staff will be very frustrated, especially on overnight events."

Wayne Stuart, former Junior Varsity Director for Central Coast YFC, from the "Campus Life/JV Newsletter."

Be Flexible
Your *real* boundaries will surface when you are with your young people. Effective crowd control and discipline are essential to the success of any junior high program, but they are not ends in themselves. During the year you may see that some rules have to be altered and some boundaries moved, because either they weren't realistic or effective, or they were counterproductive. Hard-line discipline should be used when the trusting relationship is violated; but we want kids to learn how to handle responsibilities and how to control themselves.

Your rules aren't written in stone, so be flexible and willing to change if you should.

Although discipline of young people will involve all aspects of your ministry, from this point on we will focus on meetings and events. Many of these principles can be transferred to situations with individuals.

STAGE ONE—BEFORE THE MEETING
As you plan any event, it is important to think it through, trying to spot behavioral problems before they happen. The mix of person

alities may be volatile; the setting may contribute to noise and disruptions; or the activity itself may self-destruct because of its design or contents. Think through the following:

1. *Possible Troublemakers*

Will those who have a history of causing trouble be there? (e.g., Kevin the bully, Jennifer the talker, and/or "potty mouth" Matt) Or will there be a troublesome combination of kids? (e.g., Bryan and Kenny got into a fight last week at school; Betsy isn't speaking to Carol; Tricia always seems to get on Andrea's nerves.) If so, how will you handle them? Of course you can't always know the current interpersonal conflicts or who will show up. But when you do know, be prepared.

Speak to each person individually, greeting them by name. This way you are telling them, "I know you're here today. You don't have to prove it during the meeting."

Sometimes just the predominance of a certain group of kids can cause problems. In one of my high school Campus Life clubs, a large number of seniors would regularly attend. But the real leadership in the group was in the junior class, where there were many Christian kids and student leaders. The two groups seemed to get along, so there shouldn't have been many problems. But I soon found my juniors acting up and disrupting the meetings. I was confused until I realized that subconsciously the juniors had to prove that they were the insiders and the real leaders of the group. I was able to curb the problem by talking with some of them privately and enlisting their help in keeping the meetings on track.

Also, before you start the meeting, you may want to move some individuals to better locations. Some can't help themselves when they are by certain kids.

2. *The Meeting Place*

Are there any physical aspects of the room that may contribute to crowd control problems? Some of these you will be able to change, and others you will have to learn to live with. Either way, thinking about them ahead of time will help you prepare for the worst.

For example, a room with a tile or cement floor tends to be quite noisy. That's because the accoustics are poor, and the kids are uncomfortable if they have to sit on the floor. And if they sit in chairs, the sound of the chairs scraping on the floor can be maddening. This particular problem can be corrected by changing rooms, bringing carpet squares or pillows to sit on, or giving kids a chance to move around more during the meeting.

Lighting can also be a help or a hindrance. The front of the room, where the leader stands or sits, should be well lit. This will help keep everyone's attention focused. If the leader speaks from the shadows, it will be easier for kids to stop listening.

If you have a youth room at church, you can design it for minimal problems and maximum effectiveness. But if you meet in homes, you should visit them before the meeting so you'll know what to expect. Then get there about half an hour beforehand to make the necessary changes.

Here are some guidelines to follow when considering the location. Most host parents will gladly cooperate if you let them know far enough in advance.

● Do not allow pets and younger children in the meeting. Nothing will divert kids' attention like a cute baby or puppy that has wandered into the room.

● Make sure the radio and television cannot be heard in your meeting room. In fact, don't even have it turned on in the room beforehand. Kids will get into a show and want to leave it on; and if they can hear a show or a favorite song in another room, they will talk about it—immediately.

● Do not allow the preparation of the refreshments to be a distraction. Sometimes parents will have candy and other snack foods in bowls around the room. That's a mistake. Kids will spend more time passing the bowls and eating (and throwing the M & M's) than listening. And there's nothing more distracting than hearing soft drinks being poured in the next room or hearing and smelling the popcorn as it is being popped in the kitchen.

● Choose a room that is conducive for what you have planned (and vice versa). In other words, if your crowdbreakers need space and involve a lot of moving around, don't try to do them in a small room. Choose a room that is big enough for your crowd. Junior highers don't appreciate being wedged together, especially when they have to sit next to "certain" kids. You don't want a huge room for a tiny group, but you do want them to feel comfortable. In the meeting, don't allow anyone to lie down.

● If possible, push sofas to the wall and remove the rest of the furniture from the room, especially the breakables. You probably will need the space; and remember, kids will sit on anything (even coffee tables).

● Choose a front for the meeting that is opposite the entrance and the refreshment area, with a wall behind you (not a window). This is where you will run the meeting. You should be able to see everyone from that spot. In other words, don't allow kids to sit behind you or behind chairs, couches, and so forth, or in stairways or alcoves. In fact, don't let kids sit behind anything or anybody, or turn their backs to you. If they can't see you, they think you can't see them.

● Think about other possible distractions. As you check out the room, look for anything that can cause a problem (e.g., children's toys, firewood, stack of magazines, records, tapes, souvenirs, etc.).

Our church meets in a local high school, and the Sunday School uses classrooms—complete with the teachers' desks piled high with test papers, stacks of textbooks, maps and posters on the walls, and other miscellaneous trappings of school. Besides all the obvious potential distractions, we found that our junior high kids didn't appreciate meeting in that setting because Sunday School reminded them too much of school. At first we tried to remedy the situation by pulling the chairs in a circle. We also tried having everyone sit on the floor. But the solution that worked the best was to move the class to a hallway. Everyone brings a chair (the floor is carpeted), and I provide clipboards and pencils for any writing that has to be done. The class is much more attentive and cooperative.

In that particular situation, the classroom itself was a distraction.

3. *Attention Span*

Because the attention span of junior highers is short, analyze the program to make sure it will hold their attention. If you spot possible lulls in the action, change the program or decide how you will keep everyone interested during the slower times.

> Recently I sat as an observer in the back of a junior high Sunday School class. There were eight kids, a teacher, and an adult helper. The lesson for that Sunday centered on worksheets that the teacher distributed. Here's how the class responded:
>
> • Three kids made paper airplanes with the worksheets;
>
> • One girl poked holes in her paper, in a circular pattern, until the paper fell apart;
>
> • A sixth-grade girl put the worksheet on her desk, put her head down on her arm on top of the paper, and closed her eyes;
>
> • An eighth-grade boy rolled the paper up like a telescope and looked at the teacher through it—then he stuck his pencil through the paper and twirled it in a circle;
>
> • A seventh-grader flipped the paper up into the air until it fell on the floor—then he repeated the process over and over;
>
> • An eighth-grade girl was too busy drawing a picture on another sheet of paper to notice the worksheet which lay beside her.
>
> Dave Veerman

4. *The Crowdbreakers*

Certain games and activities lend themselves to rowdiness. Because we want kids to have a good time at our meetings, many of our crowdbreakers will be of that variety. If we know what to expect, however, we will know how to head off any problems.

Are you having an eating contest? What will you do with the

peels, leftover food, or "used" marshmallows? Is the game sloppy? How will kids clean up? Does the race get everyone hot, sweaty, and wound up? How will you cool them off and calm them down?

A couple of college guys came to our Campus Life office and asked if they could run a version of Campus Life for the junior high school in their neighborhood. We gave them our blessing and a few suggestions (but not a lot of guidance). Their first activity was a pillow fight, in the school gym. Hundreds of kids showed up, and before too long, feathers were everywhere. For months afterward, feathers were blown out of the heating ducts. Needless to say, the school never forgot us. We, and our well-motivated, enthusiastic, college volunteers had not thought through the crowd control implications of the activity.

Also, be sure to have your props handy so you won't have to take time to get them together. And after a game, have a staff person pick up anything that can be broken, torn, flipped, popped, or thrown.

5. *The Discussion and Wrap-up*
We covered this in chapter 8, so I won't repeat myself, but this is where most discipline problems occur. It's not easy to get the group to calm down and get serious, and every noise and movement seems to be magnified.

It may be that you're trying to have a discussion and someone keeps acting up; you pass out worksheets, but Tanya and Paul tear them up before they are all distributed; or you want to give a short wrap-up, but no one is paying attention. What can you do to head off these problems before they occur?

This is where staff placement is especially important. They can assist kids with their work and help keep order. Make sure that they are prepared to get in place at this time in the meeting.

6. *The Refreshments*
It's usually not a good idea just to dismiss everyone and send them to refreshments. Often that will cause a stampede. At one of our youth group meetings, the boys got to the food first and ate all the donuts.

180

ORRInstead, think of an orderly way for everyone to be served. You
could have them go by teams (winning team first), or you could
have staff members posted at key locations. Tell everyone how and
where to get in line and explain that they should take only one
(drink, piece of pizza, sandwich, cup of popcorn, etc.) until everyone has been served.

By thinking ahead and anticipating potential trouble spots before
the meeting, you will be able to prevent most discipline problems.

STAGE TWO—DURING THE MEETING
1. *Give Clear Ground Rules*
As we have discussed earlier, junior highers are used to being told
what to do and usually will respect authority. They expect you to
have rules and guidelines. But they need to be told beforehand
what those rules are. Explain clearly and seriously what you expect
and the consequences of misbehaving. They should know the limits and that they will be enforced.

At camp, the main rules should be outlined during the first large
group meeting. In a Sunday School class you may want to repeat
the general rules at certain points during the year (at least once
every quarter). One Sunday School teacher led a discussion of the
rules that the class felt they should have for their time together.
After they agreed on the list, he wrote the rules on a piece of poster
board that he hung on the wall.

At these times, the enforcement procedures and consequences
should also be explained. (Put this in writing and give copies to the
parents.)

There are also special guidelines that should be explained during
most or all of the meetings, either because of a unique activity or
because kids need to be reminded. For example, in the high school
Campus Life meetings, before every discussion, I would say something like: "As you know, during these discussions we have a few
simple rules. First, you raise your hand and then speak when I call
on you; second, only one person speaks at a time; and third, you
may use no offensive language or put-downs."

When you explain the rules, ask for their cooperation and obe-
dience; don't demand it. Be positive and explicit, and remember

Behavior Management

"Unwanted behavior can be avoided through proper understanding of what causes it. The following list contains questions to ask about your own behavior and how it might help you control undesirable behavior in your kids.

1. Do I know my students individually?
2. What have I done recently to help build the self-esteem of the kids?
3. Are my students involved in the meeting? Have I given them responsibility? Have they had a part in the formation of guidelines? planning? activities?
4. Have I shown love and acceptance toward each person?
5. What expressions of praise and encouragement have I used?
6. Am I aware of my kids' interests as I plan activities?
7. What different media have I used in the past? Which could I use in the future?
8. What might be the reasons for past unwanted behavior?
9. How do I allow for individual creativity?
10. In what ways do I stimulate 'right brain' students?
11. Could I stand to change something about my appearance?
12. What is the most effective use of the room arrangement?
13. What do I have ready for the first arrival each week?"

Nancy McGuirk, adapted from *Managing Unwanted Classroom Behavior.*

that relationships will help in crowd control and discipline. The best crowd control is done by the kids themselves. Work at building the loyalties of a core group of kids who will stand behind you.

2. *Take Fast Action*
When you are confronted with a problem, respond immediately. Don't ignore it or hope it will disappear.

With an individual, be firm and confrontive, but not pushy. Keep your cool and don't ridicule or talk down to him. Also, warn the person only once. Then if he misbehaves again, take action. Here are some possible ways to respond to minor infractions (e.g., excessive whispering, poking a friend, tearing paper, untying someone's shoes, etc.):
- Address the person by name and say, "That is not acceptable. The next time it happens, I will have to _____."
- Have a staff member sit next to the person.
- Have a staff member put a hand on that person's shoulder and ask him to settle down.
- Move the offender to another part of the room, or next to you.

If the individual continues to misbehave or the problem is more serious (e.g., talking back, cheating, swearing, pushing, hitting, verbal abuse, etc.), have one of the staff members take him out of the room to talk things over.

During that talk, the staff person should ask the individual if he knows why he had to leave the room. If he will not admit that what he did was wrong, the staff person should say, "Here's what I saw you do. . . . "

Next, the staff person should ask: "Is what you were doing disruptive to or distracting from what the group is doing?" If the young person says "no" or tries to minimize the behavior, the staff person should explain that, in his opinion, it is disruptive.

Next, the staff person should ask: "Is what you were doing against our rules?" and "Can we allow you to continue doing that?" If the person doesn't see that what he did was so bad, the staff person should explain that what he did *is* against the rules and cannot be allowed to continue.

Finally, the staff person should ask, "Are you willing to work it out?" If the young person is cooperative, then the two of them should come to an understanding of what can be done to improve the situation and what will happen if it doesn't improve.

If this doesn't prove to be effective with a young person and he continues to disobey and disrupt, you should bring his parents into the situation.

Whatever you do, DON'T use physical punishment (e.g., spanking, hitting, shoving, etc.). This will hurt your ministry in more ways than I can cover here. A touch or a firm grip will say that you mean business.

With the group, the best way to respond to a problem is to use the good will of the whole group as positive peer pressure. Remind them of the ground rules, and explain that you want to treat them as adults. During the discussion or wrap-up, pause, stop, or look at the floor. Speaking louder or saying "Quiet!" usually won't work. It will also be helpful to move staff to trouble spots.

Incentives work well with junior highers and can help in crowd control. That's why Campus Life/JV meetings end with "The Biggie," an exciting crowdbreaker. Kids know that they will get to "The Biggie" if they have time. And there will only be enough time if the leader doesn't have to keep getting everyone quiet and organized.

You could spend some relationship-building time with certain kids where you could talk to them about their behavior.

If the group continues to be disruptive, you may have to end the meeting early, eliminating the last activity or refreshments. This should only be done as a last resort.

Our JV club seemed to be getting out of control. Every week we spent more time dealing with noise and discipline problems. The kids weren't antagonistic—they just couldn't control themselves. Because the meetings were supposed to be 45 minutes long (then we had refreshments and the parents came to pick them up), we explained that we would have to move things along, and we tried to enlist their cooperation. But one night, I had had enough. Right in the middle of another staff person's talk, I announced that the meeting was over and that everyone had to get their coats and leave. There was no time for refreshments—some of the parents were already outside. The kids were stunned by the abruptness of my announcement, and they left in serious silence. The subsequent meetings were much easier to control.

3. *Use Positive Reinforcement*
Discipline should not be limited to correcting negative actions. When kids do what is right, praise them. In fact, look for ways to compliment young people, publicly and privately. You can show approval for what they are doing by saying something, patting them on the back, or just giving them a knowing nod or wink. And you could reward a kid who makes progress, with a special activity.

Reinforcement

"Provide reinforcement for those who obey. Students who have a high need for attention learn that it is often easier to get attention through misbehavior than through compliance. Giving attention through the use of praise or even tangible rewards will communicate that good behavior does have a 'payoff.' "

From "Follow Me" by Tom Sawyer, Fall 1987.

This is very important with those who have caused problems in the past and are showing improvement. After a meeting you could say something like: "Mary, I really appreciated the way you participated in the discussion. You had a lot of good things to say." "Robert, I see real progress in the way you've been acting in youth group. Thanks for trying." "Thanks, Ernestine, for helping quiet everyone down. The younger kids look up to you—you're a leader."

You could also reward the entire group for being attentive, following through on an assignment, or doing what is right in a certain situation. Hand out candy, take them to McDonald's, hold a party, or reward them in some other way. These group rewards can also be effective as incentives (e.g., "If we _____, then we'll have a party").

STAGE THREE—AFTER THE MEETING

After every meeting or event you should have a time of evaluation with your staff. Discuss what went well, what needs improvement, and what you should do next time.

For discipline, this process is especially important. Talk through the problems, determining their causes and deciding on future actions.

Afterward it is also important to follow through with the individuals who caused the problems. Talking things over can be very helpful and can build the relationship. In certain cases, you may want to talk with the parents about what you are seeing and enlist their support. You want them on your team. You DON'T want them forming wrong conclusions about you and the group because of a casual or even hateful remark by their son or daughter.

- "Mr. Franklin, Dennis may have told you that I had to send him out of the room tonight at youth group. I wanted to let you know what happened and why I did what I did. . . ."
- "Mrs. Rose, I really like Stephanie, and I'm glad she's involved in the group. But, quite frankly, recently she's been disrupting the meetings with some of her comments. I was wondering if we could spend a little time talking about the situation and how we can work together to help her."
- "Mrs. Green, I think that you, your husband, Tony, and I should sit down soon and talk about Tony's behavior at church. You and I have talked before, but I think we should all get together, clear the air, and see what we can do to help Tony control his actions."

Evaluation and follow-through after the meeting will help prevent future discipline problems.

Discipline is vital for having an effective ministry with junior highers. Without limits, boundaries, rules, guidelines, and consequences, they will run wild. That's the way they are—young and full of energy.

When a Group Member Destroys Property

"Require young people to repair, clean up, or pay for the damage they have done—and more. For instance, if a young person writes on a wall, he should be required to wash all the walls in the room. If a student sticks gum under her chair, she should be required to scrape off all the gum in the room. If a kid breaks a window, he should pay for it. The young person will have to work out a way to pay back damages. This can be paid in cash or the expense for repairs could be worked off—perhaps earning $5.00 an hour by doing work around the church."

From *When You Have to Draw the Line* by Les Christie (Wheaton, Ill.: Victor Books, 1988).

Discipline is also a part of ministry itself. As positive action, it teaches young people self-control and guides them toward maturity.

Don't be afraid to exercise your authority, define your boundaries, and enforce the rules. Kids need it and expect it.

THINK IT THROUGH

1. Who or what helped you become self-disciplined?

2. What is there about your regular (or typical) meeting place that contributes to crowd control problems? What can you do to correct or minimize those features?

3. Who in your group usually causes discipline problems in your meetings? Why do you think each of these individuals acts that way?

4. How might your ministry team work together to minimize crowd control problems?

5. What would you do if a young person became a persistent troublemaker?

6. What signs do you see that some of your kids are maturing and starting to become self-disciplined?

CHAPTER 12

INVISIBLE KIDS

"Doctor, doctor!" shouted the nurse, her voice filled with breathless excitement. "There's an invisible man in the waiting room!"

Calmly the doctor replied: "Tell him I can't see him."

We may chuckle at a corny joke like that because we know that invisible people don't exist.

Or do they?

"Invisible" simply means something that is out of sight and not seen. And often we can be "blind" to things all around us. They are there, but they are out of our sight.

Thus, for all practical purposes, they are invisible. Some time ago, I had heard that mini-vans were selling well, but I hadn't really noticed. When I was thinking about buying one, however, I saw them everywhere. When I was hospitalized for a kidney stone, I thought my condition was rare. But soon it seemed as though everybody I met had suffered through one of those excruciating attacks.

Mini-vans and kidney stones had been in my world, but

189

I hadn't noticed. Then, sensitized by personal involvement, my eyes were opened. *Lack of personal involvement can limit our perspective.*

Things and people can also be invisible to us because we're too busy to see. Preoccupied with schedule and goals, we rush through our hectic lives with tunnel vision. Everything on the periphery blurs.

I remember wondering how I could have been so blind to a certain friend's need. Looking back, it was obvious that his body language, his actions, and even his words were shouting "help!" But I didn't see or hear the signs. My thoughts and concentration were elsewhere and not on him. *Life's busyness can block our vision.*

But invisibility also can come from an act of the will—a conscious choice to look the other way.

A line in Bob Dylan's classic song, "Blowin' in the Wind," states: "How many times can a man turn his head, pretending he just doesn't see?" I don't know how many times that happens, but I do know that it happens often. Faced with needy people in a hurting world, men and women turn away and act as though nothing's wrong. They pretend that the problem doesn't exist, or hope that it will go away. *Choosing to look away also determines what we see.*

I bring up invisibility because I am concerned about "invisible kids"—young men and women who are passed over, neglected, and avoided—early adolescents.

Early in this book, I explained how adults heap attention on little children, watching with wonder the miracle of growth and praising their progress. But junior highers aren't cute anymore. In fact, many of them are downright homely, awkward, and obnoxious, as they grow in fits and starts through those "wonder" years. They need affirmation more than ever, but they have become invisible.

At the other end of the continuum, we hire a professional to work with the high schoolers. With a wonderful array of exciting programs, activities, events, and trips, a full-orbed ministry hums through the year like a well-oiled machine. Even the church budget can ignore this age-group, leapfrogging over the invisible kids.

But at this time in their young lives, they need the love and concern—the ministry—of caring adults. Growing rapidly in all areas, they need support and acceptance. Learning to think and evaluate, they need answers. Making critical choices, they need guidance. Facing pressures and temptations, they need strength and encouragement. And in all of this, they need Christ.

This book has been written to open your eyes to these invisible young people—to motivate and mobilize you to reach out to kids before high school.

We have looked at the need for the ministry and the characteristics of early adolescents. We have discussed the planning process, the role of parents, and building the ministry team. We have considered how to build relationships, share the Gospel, and run meetings. And we have learned how to teach life skills and the Bible and how to discipline.

In addition, in each chapter I have included "Think It Through," a worksheet for personal analysis and ministry strategy. I hope you've taken time to answer the questions thoughtfully and honestly.

But now the reading and writing are finished—it's time to move out and move into their world. It's time for action—to reach kids and to share the vision with others. And as you minister, find a mentor, someone with ministry experience who can encourage and challenge you.

For whatever reason, don't turn off or turn away from this generation. They shouldn't be "invisible kids."

RESOURCES

YOUTH MINISTRY TRAINING OPPORTUNITIES

Dynamic Communicators Workshop
Ken Davis/DCW, 6080 W. 82nd Drive, Arvada, CO 80003, (303) 425-1319.
Taught by "Mr. Dynamic Communicator" himself (and others), these workshops train adults in the fine art of speaking, especially to youth. They are held at a variety of locations.

Group Publishing
Box 481, Loveland, CO 80539, (303) 669-3836.
Group offers many fine training opportunities, including one-day events and Youth Ministry University (which runs for about a week).

The National Institute of Youth Ministry
P.O. Box 4374, San Clemente, CA 92672, (714) 498-4418.
This organization's goal is to train, equip, and assist youth workers to have a more effective ministry with youth and their families. Programs include two-week training courses (with a maximum of twenty-four people in each course) and a series of two-day "Intensives" across the country.

Sonlife Ministries
820 North LaSalle Drive, Chicago, IL 60610, 1-800-621-7105 or (312) 329-4160 in Illinois.
A ministry of Moody Bible Institute, Sonlife's stated purpose is: "Helping the local church reach and disciple for Jesus Christ." They offer a variety of seminars including: "Principles of Ministry," "Counseling and Relationship Skills," "Principles of Ministry Training," and "Principles of Evangelism." Seminars are offered at key locations and on tape.

Youth for Christ/USA
Box 419, Wheaton, IL 60189, (708) 668-6600.

Every summer, YFC trains its new staff and other youth workers at their Summer Institute of Youth Evangelism. The schedule includes a junior high track for those specializing in that ministry. YFC also has Campus Life/JV training videos available.

Youth Specialties

1224 Greenfield Drive, El Cajon, CA 92021, (619) 440-2333.
Besides publishing many fine resources, this youth ministry organization sponsors National Youth Worker Conventions and one-day National Resource Seminars all across America.

Note: All of these seminars carry a healthy price tag, but they're worth it. When you call or write, be sure to ask about the junior high ministry courses.

YOUTH MINISTRY BOOKS AND JOURNALS

Benson, Warren S., and Mark H. Senter III, eds. *The Complete Book of Youth Ministry.* Chicago, Ill.: Moody Press, 1989.
This volume has 33 articles written by various youth experts, covering all phases of youth ministry.

Burns, Jim. *The Youth Builder.* Eugene, Ore.: Harvest House Publishers, 1988.
In this book, Jim has drawn on his experience as a veteran youth minister and has given us an excellent resource for planning, organizing, and implementing a church youth ministry. It is comprehensive, covering everything from understanding relational youth ministry to building relationships and planning programs.

Christie, Les. *When You Have to Draw the Line.* Wheaton, Ill.: Victor Books, 1988.
As we discussed in chapter 11, discipline is a critical area in working with early adolescents. This book gives a wealth of practical help for dealing with young people of all ages, including how to be a positive disciplinarian, how to deal with

anger, how to get rid of distractions, and how to deal with specialized problems.

Dausey, Gary, ed. *The Youth Leader's Source Book.* Grand Rapids, Mich.: Zondervan Publishing House, 1983.
Drawing on the wisdom of a number of youth experts, Gary provides us with a complete view of youth ministry. More than philosophy, this book gives practical ideas for building a foundation, developing an environment, planning activities, and sharpening skills.

Davis, Ken. *How to Speak to Youth . . . and Keep Them Awake at the Same Time.* Loveland, Colo.: Group Books, 1986.
One of the best youth speakers in America, Ken offers guidelines and a step-by-step approach for preparing and delivering talks to young people.

Olson, Keith. *Counseling Teenagers.* Loveland, Colo.: Group Books, 1984.
This is an exhaustive reference work for counseling, covering a multitude of problems and situations.

Spotts, Dwight, and David Veerman. *Reaching Out to Troubled Youth.* Wheaton, Ill.: Victor Books, 1987.
This book is written for Christian adults who care about troubled young people and want to reach them for Christ. The chapters on "Disciplining Troubled Youth," "Handling Problem Situations," "Getting Troubled Youth into the Church," and "Handling Special Problems" would be very helpful for junior high ministry.

Strommen, Merton P. and A. Irene. *Five Cries of Parents.* San Francisco, Calif.: Harper and Row, 1985.
Written as a result of an extensive study of early adolescents and their parents by the Search Institute, this book provides a wealth of in-depth information for both youth workers and parents. Each chapter analyzes the data, draws conclusions about

the needs of youth and parents, and gives practical advice for building a more satisfying life together.

Veerman, David. *Youth Evangelism.* Wheaton, Ill.: Victor Books, 1988.
This book is about reaching kids for Christ, and it is written for Christian adults, not just professional youth workers. Beginning with a vivid description of youth culture, it moves quickly to the practical issues of making contact, building relationships, and sharing the Gospel. The principles and guidelines in this book may be adapted to junior high ministry.

Youth Worker Journal. El Cajon, Calif.: Youth Specialties.
Although written for professional youth workers, most of whom work with senior highers, each issue of this quarterly journal contains much that applies to junior high ministry. "Focus on Junior High" is a regular column.

Note: The publishers of these books offer many other outstanding youth ministry books.

SUNDAY SCHOOL CURRICULA

Each of the Christian curricula publishing companies has a line of curriculum for junior highers or "young teens." The lessons are helpful because they are Bible oriented, they give the teacher guidance, they provide a number of resources, and they usually include teaching suggestions and information about young people. The problem with most of the lessons, however, is that they tend to use a lot of paper (worksheets for the students to use in class), try to cover too much, and are often very conceptual. So I recommend that teachers use the curriculum as a guide and a resource, and not follow it verbatim. Whatever material you choose will be most effective if it is adapted to your class and slanted to meet the needs of junior high kids.

The evangelical curricula publishing companies include:

Scripture Press — 1825 College Avenue, Wheaton, IL 60187, (708) 668-6000

David C. Cook—850 N. Grove Avenue, Elgin, IL 60120, (708) 741-2400

Gospel Light—2300 Knoll Drive, Ventura, CA 93003, 1-800-446-7735

Standard Publishing Company—8121 Hamilton Avenue, Cincinnati, OH 45231, 1-800-543-1353

There are also many fine denominational publishers. All of these companies will be happy to send you a catalog and a sample of their material upon request.

YOUTH GROUP MEETINGS AND IDEAS

"Any Old Time" Series. (Wheaton, Ill.: Victor Books.)
There are 12 volumes in this line (written, compiled, and edited by a variety of authors), each one containing 15 ready-to-use meetings. Although the target audience is high school, each meeting contains a very helpful junior high adaptation.

Campus Life/JV—Years 1, 2, and 3. (Wheaton, Ill.: Youth for Christ/USA, 1987, 1988, and 1989, respectively.)
Each volume contains twenty-five meetings, five large events, and other ideas and ministry helps. This is a life skills-oriented curriculum designed to reach the broad spectrum of early adolescents. It was written for the junior high ministry of Youth for Christ. Use the materials in your neighborhood to reach un-churched young people, or adapt the lessons for your church group. These books are not available in bookstores. Write to Youth for Christ/USA, Box 419, Wheaton, IL 60189. Or call (708) 668-6600.

Group Publishing
This publisher offers several books of games, activities, and ideas including *Quick Crowdbreakers and Games* and *Do It— Active Learning in Youth Ministry*. Be sure to choose only those activities that will work well with junior highers.

Harvest House Publishers
1075 Arrowsmith, Eugene, OR 97402, (503) 343-0123

This publisher has a series of workbooks on practical subjects called the LifeSources series. These have been written for junior and senior high school students.

Junior High Ministry. (Loveland, Colo.: Group Publishing.)
Published bi-monthly, this magazine is geared directly to junior high ministry. Each issue contains helpful articles and ideas and several meeting plans.

Serious Fun and ***More Serious Fun*** by David Veerman. (Wheaton, Ill.: Victor Books, 1987 and 1988, respectively.)
These are resource books, packed with crowdbreakers, discussion starters, discussions, and Bible studies, and organized by subject (such as identity, God, prayer, family, sex and dating, etc.). Each volume contains literally hundreds of activities. Because these books were written with high schoolers in mind, you should choose the ideas that will work well with junior highers and, specifically, with your group.

Youth Specialties
YS has an "Ideas Library" and several other books of games, crowdbreakers, skits, etc. Again, most of these are geared for high school young people, so select carefully the ones you will use.

Note: All of these publishers and organizations will be more than willing to send you a catalog of their resources upon request. In addition, many of their books can be purchased at Christian bookstores.

RESOURCES FOR PARENTS

Campbell, Ross. ***How to Really Love Your Child.*** Wheaton, Ill.: Victor Books, 1977.
In here and in the more recent *How to Really Love Your Teenager,* Dr. Campbell provides fresh insights for building parent-child relationships.

Christian Parenting Today. Sisters, Ore.: Good Family
Magazines.
As the name implies, this magazine is written for Christian par-
ents. In addition to many helpful articles, each issue has a col-
umn which discusses the junior high years. To order, write
Christian Parenting Today, P.O. Box 3850, Sisters, OR 97759.

DeMoss, Jr., Robert. ***Teen Tune-Up: A Parent's Primer on Popular Youth Culture.*** Pomona, Calif.: Focus on the Family,
1989.
This booklet contains an analysis of youth culture, including the
negative influences on youth and the family, and suggestions for
what parents can do, individually and together.

Faber, Adele, and Elaine Mazlish. ***How to Talk So Kids Will
Listen & Listen So Kids Will Talk.*** New York: Avon Books,
1982.
Although this isn't a "Christian" book, and the age range is
broader than junior high, it contains much information that parents can use in communicating with and disciplining their
children.

Focus on the Family. Pomona, Calif.: Focus on the Family.
This monthly communique from the ministry of the same name
contains helpful advice for parents and often offers resources
that parents of junior highers would find helpful. To order, write
Focus on the Family, Pomona, CA 91799.

Kesler, Jay, and Ronald A. Beers, eds. ***Parents & Teenagers.***
Wheaton, Ill.: Victor Books, 1984.
This is a comprehensive reference work with literally hundreds
of articles written by more than 70 contributors—an invaluable
resource for parents and youth workers. Because it covers the
teenage years, the material applies to older junior high students.

Kesler, Jay, Ron Beers, and LaVonne Neff, eds. ***Parents & Children.*** Wheaton, Ill.: Victor Books, 1986.

Using the same format as *Parents & Teenagers,* this book also has scores of contributors and covers just about every subject you can imagine. Much of the material relates to younger children, but chapter 14, "The Challenge of Junior High," is right on target.

McIntire, Roger. *Losing Control of Your Teenager.* Amherst, Mass.: HRD Press, 1985.
The subtitle, "Ten Rules for Raising an Adult While Keeping a Friend," tells it all. This book is about helping kids develop and mature—loving them while letting them go. Again, this is not a "Christian" book, but all parents should find it quite helpful.

Olson, Keith. *What Makes Your Teenager Tick?* Loveland, Colo.: Group Books, 1988.
Although this book focuses on teenagers (most junior highers are 11 or 12), the content will be very helpful to parents, especially those wondering how to handle a teenager in the house. Keith divides kids into eight personality types and gives insight and practical guidelines for relating to each one.

Schimmels, Cliff. *When Junior Highs Invade Your Home.* Old Tappan, N.J.: Fleming H. Revell Company, 1984.
Using a case study format, Dr. Schimmels (veteran educator and author) presents a realistic picture of junior high young people and gives practical advice for reacting to this age-group and relating to them. The book is inexpensive and easy to read—and very helpful.

Williams, Dorothy and Lyle. *Helping Your Teenager Succeed in School.* Loveland, Colo.: Group Books, 1989.
Drawing on Dorothy's work with Search Institute, Lyle's work as a junior high school counselor, and their experience as parents of three teenagers, the Williamses present friendly, practical advice to help parents help their teenagers get the most out of school.

Note: Most of the books can be found in Christian bookstores. The magazines, however, should be ordered directly from the publishers.

RESOURCES FOR KIDS

Books — Without taking time to list all the possibilities, let me just say that although there are many books on the market, I haven't found many that have solid content, are practical, and are well-written. Unfortunately, most young people don't read very much on their own; anything written for them must grab their attention. A book that you should consider is *How to Live with Your Parents without Losing Your Mind* by Ken Davis (Grand Rapids, Mich.: Zondervan Publishing House, 1988). It is a humorous and realistic book with cartoons scattered throughout.

Group Publishing also has a number of books in their "Teenage Books" line that offer helpful advice for young people. But the small print will be a barrier for younger students.

Sixth- and seventh-graders (especially girls) might find Hilda Stahl's *Elizabeth Gail* and *Teddy Jo* fiction series interesting and enjoyable (published by Tyndale House). The *Margo Mystery Adventures* by Jerry Jenkins (Moody Press), Janette Oke's stories, set in the *Little House on the Prairie* era (published by Bethany House) and *Summer Promise* by Robin Jones Gunn (Focus on the Family) are also very popular with girls.

For younger readers, the *Mandie* series by Lois Gladys Leppard (Bethany House) and the *Ivan Adventures* by Myrna Grant (Creation House) might be appropriate. Older readers might enjoy Moody Press' *Sensitive Issues* series (which includes Carole Gift Page's book, *Hallie's Secret)* and the *Cedar River Daydreams* series by Judy Baer (Bethany House).

And all of your kids should read *The Chronicles of Narnia* by C.S. Lewis.

Magazines — *Campus Life* magazine [465 Gundersen Drive, Carol Stream, IL 60188, (708) 260-6181] is written for older high school students, but eighth-graders might be able to relate. This is an outstanding publication, filled with well-written and practical articles each month. A leader's guide is also available. Consider giving one-year subscriptions to *Campus Life* to all your graduating eighth-graders.

Focus on the Family has two magazines aimed directly at junior highers. Published monthly, *Breakaway* is for boys and *Brio* is for girls. To order, write Focus on the Family, Pomona, CA 91799.

Devotionals—Again, there aren't many of these geared specifically for junior highers, but here are some that should be helpful.

- *Campus Journal.* Grand Rapids, Mich.: Radio Bible Class.

  These monthly booklets use a daily format. Each lesson gives a passage to read, an interesting narrative, questions for reflection, and a place to record personal insights. For more information, write Radio Bible Class, Grand Rapids, MI 49555.

- *Getting in Touch with God* by Jim Burns (Harvest House Publishers) and *Alive* by S. Rickley Christian (Tyndale House Publishers) are books of devotional lessons. They are written primarily for high schoolers, but many junior highers will find them quite helpful.

- *"Life Skills"* booklets. Wheaton, Ill.: Youth for Christ.

  Written by the Youth Guidance Department of Youth for Christ, these are not "devotional" booklets, but may be used as such or as follow-through materials for new Christians. *Breaking Free* tells how to "get going and start going in the Christian life"; *Stop, Look, Listen, Go* teaches how to solve problems; and *How to Get What You Need* is about communication. Each booklet contains helpful teaching and uses a workbook format. There are also many puzzles, games, and incentives to help reinforce the lessons. To order write Youth for Christ, Box 419, Wheaton, IL 60189. Or call (708) 668-6600.

- *Quietimes* by Becki Terabassi (also published as *My Daily Partner).* Wheaton, Ill.: Tyndale House.

  This notebook gives a framework and approach for personal devotions. It is designed for adding pages through the months and years and could easily be used with another resource for those who need daily guidance on what to read.

- *Youthwalk.* Atlanta, Ga.: Walk Thru the Bible Ministries.

This devotional is very well-written. Kids love the stories. Each month's colorful, mini-magazine covers a couple of life-related topics (such as "family" or "peer pressure") and relates Scripture to them. For more information, write to Walk Thru the Bible Ministries, 61 Perimeter, N.E., Atlanta, GA 30341. Or call (404) 458-9300.

Bibles—There really are no "youth" Bibles on the market today, although several make that claim. Usually these special editions are written for older kids or for young children. The closest one to junior highers is probably *The Way,* an illustrated edition of *The Living Bible.* Soon to be released, however, is the *Youth Application Bible.* Published by Tyndale House, the notes and helps in this Bible are being written by youth workers—men and women who know junior high kids. The target audience is young people, 12–15 years of age.

Note: Again, the books and Bibles should be available at Christian bookstores. But the devotional booklets and magazines should be ordered directly from the publishers.